HIKING THE OREGON COAST TRAIL

HIKING THE OREGON COAST TRAIL

(or How I Got Revenge on My Sister)

KEN PATTON

Hiking the Oregon Coast Trail: (or How I Got Revenge on My Sister)

Published by KenKinetic

Library of Congress Control Number: 2021949761

ISBN (paperback): 9781662919176
eISBN: 9781662919183

CONTENTS

INTRODUCTION

I'M BEGINNING MY new life of retirement; my last day of work was two weeks ago on June 1, 2007. During my entire working life I fantasized about having the freedom to go on a long adventure, maybe to some foreign country, maybe a bike trip across America. Many times I found myself envious of the homeless people I saw on the streets of Portland. Why? Because they had no deadlines and no performance goals. Their way of life was the opposite of the schedule-intensive, performance-based life of a professional engineer. I'm sure they would be happy to explain to me the hardships of their life, but in my eyes they appeared to have something that I craved: freedom.

During my working life, I tried to satisfy this craving with a number of little adventures. One was riding my bike down the Oregon Coast. Another was riding across Oregon into Idaho. Another was a bike tour of the San Juan Islands, and once I kayaked down the Columbia River from Portland to Astoria. I never had more than three weeks of vacation for these travels and the end of the vacation always loomed large as the days clicked by. I was getting a taste of freedom but never the whole meal. I've often wondered how many sailboats have been purchased to fulfill a fantasy of freedom, only to sit at a dock 99% of the time because the sailor's reality is a regular job.

Consistent with this dream of freedom, I have been living below my income level for many years, stashing away money so I could retire at the relatively young age of 55. And now I'm 55 and have arrived. The job is history and now it is time to live the fantasy. I'm starting relatively small, not a world tour or even a bike ride across America. This adventure is a hike down the full length of the Oregon Coast.

If you drive on Highway 101 down the coast from the Columbia River to the California border, the distance is about 360 miles. Walking the trails and beaches is a lot farther, somewhere around 460 miles if you include those acquired while wandering around lost or backtracking when the trail is blocked by high tides. This is a good "starter" adventure for a guy like me, who dreams of adventure but is actually pretty timid and not anxious to experience real adventure, which too often includes things like hunger and fear and pain and suffering. I just want to have a good time and enjoy the freedom.

It has been eleven months since my wife, Dionne, picked up the Oregon Coast Trail brochure at Fort Stevens State Park. Eleven months of planning and dreaming are coming to completion. Tomorrow it begins. Dionne and I will drive to Astoria and then on to Fort Stevens and we will walk together to the edge of the Columbia River. She will return home and I'll begin my walk along the coast to California. Fantasy will become reality.

Everything is ready. The clothes I'll be wearing in the morning are laid out. My backpack is loaded with food, water, clothes, and all of the equipment I expect to need. The weight of my pack came within ounces of my spreadsheet estimate of 24 pounds, including two pounds of water and about 5 pounds of food. That puts the base weight at 17 pounds. I'm pleased with that. I remember years ago when I took my boys backpacking, my pack weight came in at over 65 pounds. I can't imagine packing that much weight anymore. But at the time, a long hike was six miles. Now I plan on hiking somewhere around 20 miles in a day, around 400 miles total.

Will I enjoy this hike as much as I've dreamed? I hope so. It's time to find out.

HIKING ALONE

Day 1
Sunday — June 17, 2007

WHEN I STARTED the hike this morning, Dionne took my picture by the South Jetty sign, documenting my location at the mouth of the Columbia River. I had imagined that I would dip my hand in the Columbia before heading south but the jetty was fenced off for construction so I had to make do with the sign.

The hike begins.

It's been a dreary, misty, cool day. Exactly what I expected, but I would have preferred a little sunshine. I'm not complaining. It beats going to work!

The hike this morning has been all beach and all the same: the ocean on the right and a high dune with beach grass on the left. Straight ahead I can see my destination, Tillamook Head, which I could see from the minute I started the hike at 9:00 a.m. this morning. As I walk, I've been watching it very slowly growing a bit larger but it still remains a distant view.

I found some nice sand dollars but I didn't heavy my load with them. I have the company of lots of clam diggers but I'm already missing Dionne and feeling alone. After a while the hiking becomes pleasantly boring. There is no one and nothing to run into so I close my eyes and see how far I can walk before I feel like I have to open them again. I adjust my course and do it again.

I had lunch somewhere on the beach on the way to Gearhart: two pieces of pita bread, some nuts and dried apples. I put some "Randy Memorial Jam" on my pita bread. Randy was one of my running partners whose life was dedicated to running marathons on every continent. He had nearly accomplished his goal with a marathon in Antarctica scheduled when he was stricken with colon cancer and died. After his funeral his running partners all went out to breakfast together and while there I grabbed some packets of jam with the plan of using them on this hike and remembering Randy. Randy was an example to me to live life while you've got it because you never know when it will be gone.

I didn't linger over lunch today because it was getting pretty cool. My right side and the right side of my pack are wet from a mist coming off the ocean. I wouldn't mind if it was a little warmer. I called Dionne to see if she had made it home okay, and for a short time I didn't feel quite so alone. I can see Seaside ahead of me with Tillamook Head just beyond, but both are hours away.

It isn't long before I'm hungry again and the mist has cleared so that it's warm enough to take another snack break and even a short nap. I'm starting to feel the peace and relaxation that I was hoping for on this trip. When I get going again I find a young couple with a car that is stuck in the sand and I help them. Shortly after that, I find a message written in the sand, "There is healing empowering flow beside ebbing and churning H2O."

At Gearhart I hike up from the beach and begin wandering the streets, trying to find my way to the highway. It doesn't take too long to reach the Creek Side Cafe in Gearhart where I stuff myself with mashed potatoes and gravy and three pieces of fried chicken. After walking 17.5 miles I thought I'd be famished, but I had to work to eat it all and I didn't clean my plate. The folks at the restaurant were very nice and invited me to hang out as long as I wished. It was a good opportunity to get my trip journal started. It is now 5:00 and I think I'll walk another six miles this evening if I can.

View from Seaside to Tillamook Head where I'll stay the first night.

By 6:00 I've walked from Gearhart to Seaside and I am on the Seaside Boardwalk on my way to Tillamook Head. It is still a misty, dreary day. I call Dionne to let her know that I've covered 20 miles so far and that I might be losing cell coverage when I go up to Tillamook Head and probably will not talk to her again today.

When I reach the trailhead the mist is turning into a light rain, so I put on my rain gear. Not long after entering the woods, the rain ends and I have a nice dry walk through the forest.

I notice how quiet it is in the forest compared to walking on the beach, where the surf is pounding. All I can hear is the sound of a few birds singing. I'm getting tired and slow down to a mosey. It's a pretty steep climb up to the top of the head and I'm glad I have my trekking poles to help me along. By 8:00 I've reached the top. It's getting dark and there's a light rain. I cover my head with the hood of my rain jacket and let the rest of it hang over my pack. I'm feeling good, and it won't be long until I reach camp.

Tillamook Head Trail.

It's nearly dark when I make it to the campsite at a little after 9:00. The trail was getting a little hard to see as I completed my 26.5 mile hiking marathon. The camp has three little log huts, with four solid wood bunks in each one. The place was empty so I picked a cabin and laid out my stuff for the night. Then I took my food bag over to the picnic table and enjoyed an evening snack of dried apples and M&Ms while watching the rain come down. I was feeling a little lonely.

I was surprised when a couple arrived at 9:30 and then another couple arrived at 9:35. This filled the camp. Now I was lonely but not alone. In hindsight, I wish the cabins had all been occupied when I arrived, forcing me to set up my own camp further down the trail.

Clatsop Loop Trail.

Hikers Camp at Tillamook Head summit.

The campsite was very attractive but I soon learned that it had a major flaw. I went to bed at 10:00 and found the wood bunks to be very uncomfortable, even with my Thermarest pad. I eventually fell asleep but woke up at midnight with a sore neck and other body aches due to the hardness of the bed. I decided to hang my Hennessy Hammock inside the cabin. That worked great and I was soon comfortable and warm. Then the true nature of the place became apparent. I began hearing scratching noises around my equipment. Mice were getting into my stuff. I got up and moved my food bag into the hammock, but a few minutes later they were getting into the rest of my gear. As the night wore on I got short bits of sleep but the scampering feet and scratching kept waking me up. Every time I woke up I flashed my light or made a noise to scare them off. They scampered away for a bit and then came back. Finally at 4:00 in the morning I gave up, packed my gear and used my tiny LED light to hike a quarter of a mile down the trail in the dark. I found a flat spot where I lay down to get a little rest and wait for the sun to come up.

Day 2

Monday, June 18

"Not all those who wander are lost." —J.R.R. Tolkien

When the sun came up I broke my second camp and continued down the trail. I was exhausted from lack of sleep, and after just one day on the trail asked myself, "Why am I out here and not at home?" This isn't the euphoric fantasy that I had in mind when I was planning this trip. I was tired and hungry and alone with my dreary thoughts. I tried to encourage myself as I made my way down the trail. The adventure isn't about being better than home, it is about being different than home, to move out of my comfort zone and experience new things.

A couple of hours later I was hiking along a cliff and looking down at a magnificent ocean view, listening to the birds sing and saying, "This is worth it. It's Monday morning and I'm not getting ready for work. I'm not going to work. I'm hiking down a beautiful path in the forest."

After yesterday's marathon I expected my legs to be complaining, but they are doing fine. They only hurt when going uphill. Today I expect to travel about 15 miles, so they will get some rest.

As I walk down this beautiful trail I think about the team from the Lewis and Clark Corps of Discovery, who hiked here from Fort Clatsop to get whale blubber off a washed up whale. They didn't succeed because the Tillamook Tribe got to it first, leaving nothing but a skeleton. But as I walk these trails and I see all the underbrush and fallen trees, I wonder: How did they possibly walk through here? Then I realized that the tribe had built and maintained the paths that the Core of Discovery used. But that just moves the question to another level. How did they make these trails? Without a chainsaw, I couldn't imagine cutting through all these downed logs. They didn't even have steel hand tools. Maybe when I get home I'll do some research.

Indian Beach with Cape Falcon in the distance.

Indian Beach is gorgeous. I take a photo and then walk a few yards and then take another and another and another. This place is healing me. I'm in full awe of the beauty of the beach and the cliffs and the ocean and forest and the rugged rock islands. The euphoria has kicked in. The trail and the views are continuously magnificent as I walk through Ecola State Park on my way to Cannon Beach. By 8:30 I have gone six miles and have arrived in Cannon Beach, where I will find someone to make my breakfast.

It's 9:30 and I've finished a breakfast of biscuits and gravy at the Fireside Restaurant, and now I'm sitting on a public bench in Cannon Beach. I'm experiencing the inefficiencies of travel. I want to pick up a tide table and map at the information center but they don't open until 10:00. I wanted to write this entry and charge some batteries at the library but it doesn't open until 1:00 p.m. I have found a hot spot though, so I'm going to try to send out an email.

Haystack Rock.

At 10:30 I have my tide table and I'm on my way out of Cannon Beach, walking the shore that I've so often walked in the past. Dionne and I come to Cannon Beach for lots of little weekend vacations. I pass by Haystack Rock and I'm in a bit of a hurry: I've learned from the tide table that the tide is coming in and I don't have much time to get around Hug Point before the route is flooded.

When I arrive at Hug Point at noon I'm pleased to find it is high and dry. In the early 1900s, the beach was the highway and Hug Point was often a barrier even when the tide wasn't high, so they blasted out the side of the cliff and made a narrow solid rock path around the point that is always accessible except at high tide. The beach is indeed flooded, but I'm able to get around Hug Point on this rock road. On the other side of Hug Point I take a break, but maybe I shouldn't have. I might have gotten around the next point if I'd gotten to it earlier, but even with my shoes off and wading in the water I can't get by, so I have to go up on the highway.

Rock road around Hug Point.

At Arch Cape I am able to walk part of the way on back roads, which gets me off of busy Highway 101. At 2:00 I stop at a little grocery store to buy a quart of chocolate milk and drink it while I walk. A very short distance from the store, just before a tunnel, I cross the highway and take a side road to the Cape Falcon Trailhead. The trail up to the Cape starts out at a suspension bridge over Arch Cape Creek and immediately takes off uphill. That quart of chocolate milk is feeling a little heavy in my stomach so I sit down for a rest. I have hiked about 16 miles so far today and I'm finding myself in a little bit of a funk again. It's shady here and I'm thinking that when I was in the sun, I was feeling better. Are my emotions being affected by the sun? Or am I worn out and tired, or lonely? I don't know. Forty-five minutes later my funk is gone. I'm still alone and still tired, but I am in the sunshine. Maybe the calories from the chocolate milk have kicked in. I don't know.

Suspension bridge over Arch Cape Creek.

As I climb up the trail I find my energy level rising. I'm feeling good and enjoying myself. On the way up to the top of Cape Falcon I walk through a dense forest of little trees growing almost as thick as grass. It reminds me of a dark forest that Bilbo Baggins might have walked through on his Hobbit adventures.

Trail to Cape Falcon.

The sun only penetrates in tiny spots and it's like walking through a tunnel. There are no signs along this trail and I come to a number of intersections that leave me wondering which way to go. It's getting late and I'm getting tired and I really misjudged the distance I'd be hiking today. I've already gone over 20 miles and I don't feel like sightseeing anymore. I just want to get to Oswald West Park and get off my feet. At a fork in the trail I take a turn to the right when I should have turned to the left and find myself wandering around numerous trails near the tip of Cape Falcon. On the upside, I do get some fantastic views of Neahkahnie Mountain and the beach toward Cape Lookout. I wish the photos could do it justice.

Late afternoon view from Cape Falcon back to Tillamook Head where I started the day.

I finally find the trail to Oswald West at about 6:00 p.m. I follow that trail and only get sidetracked on unmarked branch trails a couple of times before reaching the campground at 7:30 p.m. The camp is a little noisy and I want to get to sleep early, so I walk another half hour beyond it and find a place off the trail to hang my hammock. What I thought would be an easy 15 mile day turned into another

26 mile marathon hike from my camp at Tillamook Head this morning. I hide from the mosquitoes in my net-covered hammock while I eat a power bar for dinner.

The day has been an emotional rollercoaster, which at the time I blamed on the sleepless night on Tillamook Head and the two long days of hiking, and maybe even a shortage of food. I don't know how to describe the low points other than I was in a funk and not enjoying myself. Then the sun would shine on me or I would have something to eat or, for no good reason at all, my mood would change and I'd feel better for a while. Fortunately the funk periods were usually short, but this was no time for any funk! I was living my dream; I was supposed to be in ecstasy!

I wasn't able to call Dionne to let her know my location because there was no signal in the area. It's always a little unnerving when I can't get in touch with her because I know she worries about me.

Stealth camp in Hennessy Hammock at the base of Neahkahnie Mountain.

Day 3
Tuesday, June 19

I had a good night's sleep last night. There were no critters or people to bother me and I'm feeling good. This morning I was packed up by 5:45 and started the day walking up the base of Neahkahnie Mountain. It was a short distance from my camp to where I crossed Highway 101. Just before reaching 101, I started to overheat on the steep climb so I set my pack down by the side of the trail and took off my jacket and base layer. I stuffed the jacket into its bag and put it between my knees so it wouldn't roll down the slope while I removed my base layer and put my shirt back on. When I loosened my pants to tuck my shirt in, the jacket bag slipped out from between my legs and started rolling. I thought it would roll to the side of the trail and stop but no, it was on its way back down the mountain. I held my loose pants up and ran down the trail chasing after the escaping jacket. It was definitely not stopping and it had a long way to go before it reached a switchback. The good news is that I was gaining on it. I couldn't reach down and grab it or I would have dropped my pants, so with one last burst of speed I jumped in front of it and the years of soccer practice with the kids paid off as I stopped it with my foot. I tucked my shirt in, fastened my pants, picked up the jacket, and hiked back up the trail to my pack, then continued on up the hill to Highway 101.

I'm feeling good this morning with no sign of yesterday's funk. It's a great day, I'm on a lovely trail, and I'm having a great time. At Highway 101, I plug the auxiliary battery pack into my phone and try to make a call, even though no bars are showing. It works and I'm able to let Dionne know where I am and tell her a little about my day before the signal drops.

The 1700-foot elevation gain to the top of Neahkahnie Mountain was a little challenging. I'm glad I decided to bring trekking poles. My legs were rebelling after two 26 mile days and the poles were very helpful on the steep trail up the side of Neahkahnie Mountain. I could have walked on the road to Manzanita but climbing the mountain was worth the effort. The view from the top is magnificent. I could see 25 miles south past Cape Meares to Cape Lookout, where I'll be camping tomorrow evening. I could also look back 15 miles north to Tillamook Head where I left "Mouse Camp" yesterday morning.

At 7:45 after walking about three miles I encounter a log across the path. I don't have the energy to crawl over it so I sit on it and take a break. I drink some water and contemplate life. I start with a pleasant thought. This is a Tuesday and I could be at work today but I'm not, and this isn't just a vacation, I'm never going back to work. This is my life now, this and whatever else I want to do, and that makes me happy, plus the fact that the sun is shining through the trees and the path is beautiful and the sky is clear and it is a gorgeous day. I quit contemplating life when I have the energy to get over the log. Forty-five minutes later I'm at the summit and I take a photo of the spectacular view south to Cape Meares, and beyond that to Cape Lookout. I won't arrive at Cape Lookout for days. I think I can see maybe 50 miles to the south.

View of Manzanita, Neahkahnie Beach, Nehalem Bay, Cape Meares,
and in the far distance, Cape Lookout.

I had visualized making myself some breakfast at the summit but it isn't that far to Manzanita now and maybe someone there will make me some pancakes and eggs. That would be much better than a cup of cold oatmeal. As you may have noticed, I don't cook anything. I have chosen to lighten my load by not carrying a stove or fuel or pots and pans. I figure a power bar or some pita bread and jam will usually get me to the next restaurant.

On the way down Neahkahnie Mountain I met a man on his way up. He was the first person I'd seen on the trail in two days. It isn't that I haven't seen lots of people in parks and in towns, just not on the trails. He was winded and having a hard time so he was happy to stop and chat. He wasn't sure he was on the right trail and I was able to tell him he was and how much farther he had to go to get to the top. Then he asked me where I had hiked from. When I told him I started at the Columbia River he said "Wow, I wish I would have done something like that when I was younger." I asked, "How old are you?" And he said, "I'm 55." "I'm 55 too," I said. "If you train for a while you can get in shape and do it." "No," he said, "I'm too old and out of shape." I hope he'll see the view up there and change his mind.

I met a young couple at the base of the trail, and when they saw my pack they asked me where I was headed. I told them my story and the man said, "How do you do that? How do you find the time?" It gave me the opportunity to preach my gospel of living below your means and not buying boats and RVs and saving that money to retire young so you can do things like this. He said, "Yeah, my dad hasn't saved anything and he'll be way too old when he retires to do anything like this, and I'm headed that direction too." So I encouraged him to give it a try and he said he thought it was a pretty interesting concept. I hope I was able to help him.

It's a short walk on the road to Manzanita and I arrive there just before noon. My feet are starting to hurt a little and I think I'm developing a blister. In Manzanita I fuel up with eggs, pancakes, and bacon. I call the Jetty Fishery and make arrangements to have them take me across the mouth of Nehalem Bay this evening at 7:00.

I stop at Nehalem Bay State Park to take a shower and clean my stuff and organize things. It's 4:00 now and I need to leave here at 4:30 to meet the boat at the mouth of Nehalem Bay at 7:00. For $10 they will take me across the Bay to the south jetty, where I can continue my hike. Some of the clothes I've washed may not be dry in time. I check my feet and definitely have a blister developing on my left little toe.

I left the park in the late afternoon and had a nice leisurely walk on the beach to the north jetty. I'm enjoying the sunshine; there are just a few clouds in the sky and a light breeze is coming off the ocean. I'm having a great time. I had no problem getting to the north jetty in time for the 7:00 pick-up. In fact, I was there at 6:00. I walked east on the jetty to a point straight across from the marina in hopes of signaling them for an early pickup. Fifteen minutes later I was waving a red handkerchief in the air to get the attention of a couple of guys on the dock. No response. I put the red handkerchief on a long stick and waved that. No response. Were they ignoring me, or were they just not looking? I could see them perfectly well. I was sure they could see me. At 6:45 I started blowing my whistle while I waved. That worked. One of the guys on the dock waved back, mimicking my wave. Then he waved his arms out to the side and I waved my arms out to the side mimicking his wave. Then I waved my arms in circles and he waved his arms in circles. Was he toying with me or was he really going to bring a boat over? Then he waved his arms in the air and swung one leg up and down and yes, I responded likewise. Then he did semaphore signals. At this point I dropped out of the game and with a sigh of relief saw another guy maneuver a boat out from the dock and head my way.

My ride across Nehalem Bay.

It was a little aluminum fishing boat but the water was shallow and he couldn't get within fifteen feet of the shore. I took my shoes and socks off and waded out to the boat and hopped in. His prop got stuck in the sand so I took my backpack off and jumped back in the water to give the boat a push out. By the time I was back in the boat the current had carried us back into the sand. This time instead of getting out, I extended one of my trekking poles and used it to push us off the bottom and out into the channel.

Once safely in the boat and on our way across the channel, I thanked my chauffeur for coming to pick me up before the scheduled time. He said that no one had told him that he was supposed to pick up a hiker. He just came because he saw me waving at him.

When we got to the marina the fellow I had exchanged signals with helped me out of the boat. He was just a kid, maybe 18 years old, having a good time with a hiker. He said he hadn't seen me at all until I whistled. When I looked across the channel I could understand why. The sun was low in the sky right behind where I was standing and it was hard to see anything over there against the glare of the sun.

The high tide kept me from walking the south jetty out to the beach. The choices were the highway or the railroad tracks and I chose the tracks. I can't tell how far I followed them because my pedometer got wet in the boat when I took my backpack off. It was ruined.

Walking the rails back to the beach.

I got off of the tracks at the first road heading west. In a short time I was on the beach walking south. I was surprised at how good my legs and feet were doing. I felt like I could walk forever. At 8:00 I stopped to eat a piece of pita bread and some snacks and then walked another hour as the sun was nearing the western horizon. This is my third night on the trail and the first chance to see a sunset. I'm still walking as the sun goes down. As the sky darkens I find a nice log where I sit for a while before setting up camp on the beach.

I messed with the auxiliary battery pack for my phone and discovered that if I held the connector at just the right angle I could get it to charge the phone. After holding it in that position for about fifteen minutes, I had enough of a charge to call Dionne and let her know that I'm very near Twin Rocks. The battery held out and we had a nice long talk. I was missing her. She should be with me. In fact, the idea for this walk was originally hers, but since she hasn't retired from her job yet, I'm out here alone. For now.

My view while sitting on the beach waiting for the sun to go down before setting up my stealth camp.

Combining the distance trekked before the pedometer was ruined and the amount of time I walked after that, I estimated that I had traveled about 21 miles today, for a trip total of 74 miles. I sat on the log until well after sunset and watched the stars and moon appear in the night sky.

At 10:00 the darkness was sufficient to hide me so I set up my beach camp, which consisted of a 4ft x 7ft Mylar sheet on the ground with my Thermarest pad on top of it and my one-pound sleeping bag on top of that. I thought of setting up my hammock as a tent but decided it would be nice to see the stars in the cloudless sky. It is a beautiful evening and I can see the moon and one of the planets, and the stars are just beginning to appear.

Day 4
Wednesday, June 2
Lost in Garibaldi

It was nice to see the stars but there was a price to be paid. My little ground cloth wasn't large enough to keep the sand from coming over the edges and getting all over everything, and since I had nothing to protect me from the ocean breeze, I was cold most of the night.

At 2:00 a.m. I pulled the Hennessy Hammock out of the bag and used it as a blanket, which helped a little. By 4:45 I knew I wouldn't be able to sleep anymore and I knew I would be warmer if I was walking, so I broke camp and headed south on the beach. A crow walked along the beach with me for quite a while, staying about fifteen feet to my right. Maybe he was trying to give me a little company and encouragement on my walk. Maybe he was hungry and looking for a handout. I was hungry and looking forward to finding a place to have breakfast in Garibaldi.

It was high tide and I soon found my way blocked by a rock outcropping that extended about twenty feet into the ocean. I looked for a way over it but the cliff looked dangerous and no trespassing signs were posted all over the place, so I returned north about half a mile to a spot where I could leave the beach and continue my hike on Highway 101. I got on the highway at the Twin Rocks Friends Camp about 4 miles north of Garibaldi, and I would walk on 101 for the rest of the day. I wasn't on the road long when I had to break my safety rule of always walking against the flow of traffic. When I started walking on the left-hand side of the road, I found that the curves in the road around cliffs on the east side of the highway hid the oncoming cars and trucks from view. Drivers tended to cut the corners and encroach on the shoulder where I was walking, so I decided to walk on the right side of the road where the visibility was better and it afforded a better view of the channel into Tillamook Bay. There are a number of scenic rock islands very near the road.

I was hungry and anxious to find a restaurant when I reached Garibaldi. About halfway through town I stopped at a service station to ask for a recommendation.

The attendant suggested I walk back to the north end of town to Fisherman's Corner at the harbor. I was almost there when I struck up a conversation with a fellow who said that Fisherman's Corner was closed on Wednesdays and that I should head back to the south end of town where I would find Penny's Parkside Café. I walked through town to Penny's, where I was told that they don't serve breakfast, and they sent me to the Garibaldi Pub and Eatery back in the center of town. After walking about a mile wandering around Garibaldi and passing this pub three times without considering having breakfast in a bar, I arrived back at the pub, right next door to the service station where I had originally asked for a recommendation. I'm glad that Garibaldi is small and walking from one end of town to another isn't a long journey. And I'm glad that I seem to have gotten beyond funks, because all this wandering around tired and hungry and sore could get depressing. But I'm doing fine. After all, it is Wednesday and I'm not at work. I was pleased with my final destination; the food was good and cheap. For four dollars plus tip I got two eggs, biscuits, and hash browns. Such a deal.

After breakfast I walked south for only a block before I had to stop. My left little toe was screaming at me. I sat on a bench, took my left shoe off and inspected my toe. It didn't look good. Most of the skin was coming off. I dabbed some antibiotic on it and wrapped it as well as I could, put my shoe back on, and started to walk again. Ouch! It hurt. I hobbled along and over the next mile the pain numbed and I picked up speed and my gait returned to normal.

At about 9:00 at an intersection just south of Garibaldi, a guy in a pickup truck offered to give me a ride. I thanked him, but told him I'm walking to California. As he drove off I pulled out my harmonica and played as I walked. Even though my toe was hurting and I was walking on the road rather than a trail or beach, I was feeling good about life. I continued on around Tillamook Bay to Bay City.

After a while I got tired of playing my harmonica and tired of cars and trucks blasting by and tired of my foot hurting and again I asked myself, "Why am I doing this?" Oops, I'm feeling another funk coming on and I'm starting to question why I'm out here again. Well maybe it's just because I can! In my working life I could only dream about doing something like this and now I can do it and I'm going to do it even if it hurts! And I'm going to do it because it's a challenge and the good times really are good and I know that a funk like this doesn't usually last very long. So shut up and quit whining!!! There, I hope that works for a while. I'll be playing my harmonica again soon.

Our friends, Andrea and Larry, live in Bay City. When I arrived there I called Larry to get directions to their house but no one answered the phone. I figured they must be out so I found a little grassy area by the city hall and rested my foot for a while. After my rest, I called again, and again got no answer. So I went into the city hall and asked them to show me on the map where the family lives and I made my way to their house. I'm glad I did. It turns out they were home but their phone wasn't working. They invited me in, fed me, and gave me the run of their house while I waited for Dionne to arrive. I'm glad today's distance was a relatively short 11 miles. My little toe needs a rest.

Dionne arrived at Andrea and Larry's place at about 5:30. Their daughter, Ginger, and her family were visiting too. When Dionne came in I smiled and greeted her. Ginger saw my expression at seeing Dionne and said, "It must be so nice to see someone's face light up when you walk in the door." I was glad she saw the joy on my face but sorry for her that she apparently didn't get that feeling from her own husband. I learned later from Andrea that Ginger and her husband were having a hard time. It reminded me of the unfulfilled hunger for affection that I had in my previous marriage. No problem with that, now that I have Dionne. I hope Ginger and her husband can work things out. *(They did.)*

It was great to see Dionne but we didn't get to have much time alone together since we were visiting with our hosts and their neighbors well into the evening. The good news is that the weekend is near and Dionne will join me again in Pacific City while I take a one day break from the walk.

Today's mileage brings the total trip distance to 85 miles; that's a little over 21 miles per day so far.

Day 5

Thursday, June 21

I'm Healed . . . and Today I Got to be a Game Warden

Last night I had the best sleep I've had in months. I went to sleep around 9:45 and didn't wake up until the alarm went off at 5:00 a.m. Dionne said I slept quietly with no sleep apnea symptoms or snoring. She slept well too. I woke up refreshed and looking forward to the day.

Just weeks before this trip I had a sleep test and was told that I had severe sleep apnea. The condition causes your airway to close when you fall asleep, which causes you to snore and also stops your breathing until your sleeping mind says "Hey! I'm suffocating!" and sends a signal to pump a little adrenalin into your system, which wakes you up, or almost wakes you up, and you gasp for air and then a few minutes later you fall asleep again and quit breathing again and wake up again and so on all night. Since you don't totally wake up, you don't even know it's happening. It is usually discovered by your sleeping partner, who lies awake listening to all this commotion.

This restless sleep can leave you pretty tired the next day, and in the long term all those little jolts of adrenaline can lead to high blood pressure, heart attack, and death. Some people get this because they are overweight. My doctor said that at five foot ten inches tall and 175 pounds, I was not overweight. My problem was more of a control problem in my brain, so I was put on a machine that pumps air through my nose all night to keep the airway open. I had been using it at home and it did solve the problem, but I sure wasn't going to pack that thing down the coast with me. I was pleased to find out from Dionne that I slept well without it.

In the process of training for this hike I lost a total of fifteen pounds which, contrary to the doctor's opinion, made a big difference in my sleep apnea. *(When the hike was over I took the machine back and haven't needed it since. I have a major incentive to keep that weight off so I don't develop sleep apnea again.)*

First on the agenda this morning was breakfast at a little restaurant in town with Dionne and Andrea and Larry. Larry had offered to take me back to Manzanita, launch his boat from there and ferry me across the channel to the peninsula so I wouldn't have to hike all the way around Tillamook Bay to get to Cape Meares. That sounded great to me, but then he got a message from his doctor concerning his heart test results and he decided that the physical effort of launching the boat wouldn't be a good idea. Instead he offered to drive me around the bay and up the peninsula as far north as the road went, which would be farther north than his home in Bay City. That worked for me. It would be no different than getting a boat ride across, and my start point today would be a little north of my endpoint yesterday so that's fair. Fair, by the way, is walking every bit of the way to California with the exception of walking on water. I haven't mastered that yet, so I consider boats across channels and car rides around bays acceptable.

After Dionne left for Portland, Larry drove me around the bay and dropped me off at 7:00. A path at the end of the road would take me across the dunes to the ocean side of the Bayocean Peninsula.

Larry (on the right) and me in front of Brownies Cafe where Andrea and Dionne joined us for breakfast before Larry drove me to Bayocean Peninsula.

The morning was great. There was a light cloud cover with a little blue sky showing and no wind. That full night of sleep did wonders for me. I felt on top of the world. My early journal entries have the question, "Why am I doing this?" I was asking the question because I wasn't enjoying the trip as much as I felt I should. It may just be that I've been sleep deprived. I got almost no sleep the first night in the mouse infested cabin, a barely adequate sleep the second night and very little sleep on the beach the third night. With a full night's rest I felt great, even though it turned out to be a challenging day. *(With full hindsight, I think the good mood was largely due to having the company of Dionne and friends.)*

I hiked the peninsula to the little town of Cape Meares and then walked through town and found the trail at the end of Fifth Street, just as my guide book described. The trail was easy, basically a gravel road. I missed a turnoff somewhere and ended up coming out on Cape Meares Loop Road instead of the lighthouse access road. It was no problem though. I just walked about a mile on the lightly traveled road up to the access turn off. I did get to stop at the same viewpoint that Dionne and I stopped at a few years ago on our 2001 bike ride down the coast. It is a great view looking north to Neahkahnie Mountain, Cape Falcon, and beyond to Tillamook Head.

Looking north to Tillamook Bay and Bayocean Peninsula.

I took my time at the lighthouse, read the information plaques, took pictures and had a snack before continuing on the trail to the Octopus Tree, which is an amazing multi-trunk spruce tree. From there I followed the trail down the south side of Cape Meares toward Oceanside.

Cape Meares Lighthouse.

Old hiker at the Octopus Tree.

The last two miles to Oceanside are on Cape Meares Loop Road, which is very quiet and easily walked. Eventually the sun burned through the clouds and I started to overheat. I took off a layer and unzipped the legs from my pants, turning them into shorts. Feeling more comfortable, I continued to enjoy the walk down the quiet road.

I was lost in thought when I became aware that I had walked to within 15 feet of a deer. I think it noticed me the same instant I noticed it. It gave a little start but didn't retreat. I slowly pulled my camera out of my pocket, expecting the deer to take off before I had a chance to take a picture, but it didn't move. It flinched a bit at the shutter sound but held its ground. We stood there looking at each other for a few more moments until it wandered away, nibbling on bushes as it went. I felt like nibbling too so I left the deer and continued on to Oceanside, feeling a little closer to nature and hoping to find lunch.

Who will blink first?

I was surprised by Oceanside. How, after all of my trips to the coast over the years, have I missed this place? I found it enchanting. I loved the way the houses were built up the hillside and the quietness of the main street and the exceptional view of the ocean and rock islands. I have to come back here sometime and bring Dionne with me.

The enchanting town of Oceanside.

An old fellow sitting on a bench outside of the post office directed me to Rosanna's Cafe. The prices were a little higher than what I was used to but I found one item that was about half the cost of anything else, biscuits and gravy with two eggs. It isn't as if I'm poor; I could easily buy anything on the menu but that wouldn't feel right. I'm a backpacker, and in the spirit of backpacking, it seems that I should be frugal. And besides, I was hungry and a meal of biscuits and gravy was appealing.

I took my time eating lunch, soaking in the atmosphere of the place and enjoying the great view out the window. The ocean was mesmerizing as the waves washed across the familiar Three Arch Rocks and the beach. This place gave me a good feeling, which added to my general sense of well being. It was a Thursday and I wasn't at work; I was sitting in a restaurant on the coast with a view of the ocean and I was in no hurry to get anywhere. I was enjoying the moment, with no sense of *needing* to enjoy the moment. I'm retired. No deadlines, no schedules, and no fear that I had to seize the moment as I'd felt on my short vacations in the past. This is no vacation, this is my new life, I thought. I can relax and let the moments come and go as they please. I have plenty of time.

Enjoying the view from Rosanna's Cafe in Oceanside.

After lunch I went down to the beach and began my two-mile walk to Netarts. Netarts is where I was facing a small challenge. I needed to find some way to get across the outlet of Netarts Bay or I'd have to walk on the road all the way around the bay to Cape Lookout.

As I approached Netarts I saw a small boat in the channel with three people in it tending crab cages, right where I wanted to cross. I waved my arms but wasn't getting their attention. I tried my whistle but that didn't seem to work either. I continued to walk along the beach and wave, hoping that at some point they would see me. After about ten minutes of waving and whistle blowing they waved back. I waved more vigorously and motioned for them to come to me and eventually they did start to come a little closer. I waved a ten dollar bill hoping they could see I was offering money, but from that distance I didn't really expect they could tell. They continued to come closer but had to stop about 200 feet from shore because the water was too shallow. Now they were close enough to hear me so I yelled that I would come out to them. I started to take my shoes and socks off to wade out but then I took a closer look at the rocks and shells and decided I'd better wear shoes. I stuffed one sock in my pocket and put the shoes back on and started wading to the boat.

As I got closer I yelled, "I'm walking to California and need a ride across the channel," as I waved the ten dollar bill in the air. Does this seem like appropriate behavior for a 55-year-old professional engineer? Well, I'm not a professional engineer anymore, I'm a traveler. I wouldn't have been surprised if they thought I was a nutcase, and maybe they would be right. Anyway, they invited me aboard and balanced the boat in preparation for my entry as I hauled myself out of the water and rolled onto the floor of their boat. I'm glad it was dry. Without hesitation, I explained my mission of walking to California. They were happy to ferry me across the channel for free but I insisted they take the ten dollars saying, "You have no idea how much this is going to help me out."

The crew was a father, mother, and daughter from Wyoming on their vacation. This was their first experience at crabbing so they weren't sure they were doing it right. When they saw me waving at them they thought I was a game warden because of the green shirt and cargo shorts I was wearing. They thought the ten dollar bill I was waving was my badge and wondered why game wardens in Oregon couldn't afford a boat and had to stand on the shore and wave at people, hoping they would come to shore.

Knowing full well at this point that I wasn't a game warden, they still wanted to show me their crabs so I could tell them if they were the right kind and the right size and gender. I told them I'd never been crabbing in my life, so they knew more about it than I did. They showed them to me anyway and the crabs looked fine to me, so I told them they should catch all they want and if anyone asks, they could tell them the game warden told them it was okay.

My ride across the channel to Netarts Spit.

They dropped me off at the south side of the channel and posed for a photo before getting back to their crab pots. The last thing I heard the father say as they motored off is, "I think that's an island." So there I was, thinking I was on the Cape Lookout spit and being told I was on an island. That would have been an interesting situation. I continued wearing my game warden uniform thinking it might come in handy if I needed to commandeer another boat to get off the island.

I hadn't walked far before I decided I needed to get my damaged left little toe out of my wet sock. I found a log to sit on and dug some dry socks out of my pack. When I took the sock off and looked at my toe I didn't like what I was seeing. The whole end of my toe looked like it was falling off; ick. I got some antiseptic out of my first aid kit and covered the exposed area. I tried to apply a blister patch but it wouldn't stick because of the antiseptic, so I wound medical tape around the blister patch and then around my foot to hold everything in place. It seemed like a pretty good job until I stuck my foot back in my shoe and tried to walk. The tape didn't allow my foot to spread as weight was put on it. My toe and foot were pinched and it hurt like . . . so I stopped after a short distance and removed the portion of tape that was wrapped around my foot. That relieved some of the pain but not much. I dealt with it for a few minutes and then stopped again and removed some more of the tape. It still hurt to walk but it seemed better to leave the last of the tape and blister patch on rather than expose the open wound to the elements. I continued to walk and eventually the pain became background noise and I began to enjoy the hike again.

The north end of the spit (and it was the end of the spit, not an island) is about five miles from Cape Lookout State Park. Other than a deer and some turkey vultures and seagulls, I had the beach all to myself all the way. It seemed to take forever to get to the campground. I think it was because the view hardly changed. There was always a high sand dune on my left and ocean on my right and no trees or islands or cliffs or anything different from one mile to the next to break the monotony or to get my mind off the pain in my foot.

Cape Lookout . . . will I ever get there?

I arrived at the park at 4:00 p.m. After registering I took a shower in the main camping area and then went to the hiker/biker area. It was not the same as I'd remembered it when Dionne and I stayed here on our bike trip. It used to be secluded and dense with trees; now it is open and the breeze off the ocean was chilling. I put on my long underwear, my shirt, my puffy jacket, and my rain jacket, and even with all that I wasn't really warm while I ate my dinner of English muffins, dried apples and nuts. Rather than sit there and freeze until bedtime I went over to the car camping area where the wind was blocked and it was much warmer.

When I got there I noticed I had a cell phone signal, and I also noticed some yurts. A yurt would be a fine improvement to my living conditions. I went back to the registration booth and they rented me the last one available, applying what I had already paid for the hiker/biker site to the $27 cost of the yurt. They confirmed that the hiker/biker area had changed. A number of trees had come down and the ocean had taken out a lot of the beach, so the water was actually much closer than it used to be.

Yurt at Cape Lookout State Park.

The inside of the yurt must have been 80 degrees. It had been heated by the sun all day with no ventilation. I'd gone from one extreme to the other. I took off a couple of layers of clothes and opened up the yurt to get some ventilation and then wandered around camp looking for the best cell phone signal. I called Dionne and we struggled through dropped signals and missing words but finally succeeded in having a conversation.

As I write this journal entry in the comfort of the yurt, it's raining outside. I'm really glad I didn't just sit over there in the hiker biker area and endure the cold. The only downside to a yurt is the close proximity of chatty neighbors. I might need to wear earplugs tonight, but I'll still get a better night's sleep than in a cold hammock.

I worked on my journal at the table inside the yurt,
using my Palm TX and keyboard.

It is getting late for this hiker, almost 10:00 and time to get to bed. I don't intend to get up early though. No reason to rush out in the morning, although I'm looking forward to reaching Pacific City. Dionne will be joining me at the Pacific City Inn sometime tomorrow evening.

Day 6
Friday, June 22

I listened to the rain falling last night and was so glad I was in a yurt. I suspect at some point on this trip I will not be so lucky. I slept in and didn't leave camp until after 7:00. On my way out of the campground I stopped at the restroom and a brief rain shower came through and was gone by the time I was cleaned up and on my way.

The trail over Cape Lookout.

The trail over Cape Lookout goes through a lush forest and there were lots of birds singing. Once in a while a rain shower came through, but not enough to put on my rain jacket. I passed on the five-mile round trip to the end of the cape and went directly down the south side. About half way down to the beach the strangest thing happened. I suddenly got multiple stings or bites on my left leg. I instantly swept my leg off with my hands and I think I saw something fly away but

I'm not sure. Whatever it was, it really stung all the way around my leg. I found three tiny red spots on my leg, one oozing a little blood. I can't imagine what it was that got me. The stinging sensation continued for hours. After putting some medication on the spots, I continued down to the beach for the long walk to Sand Lake.

The beach was very wide and empty and there was no one in sight for miles. The walk to Sand Lake was uneventful until I reached the motorized vehicle area. Swarms of four wheelers and motorcyclists sped up and down the beach and into the dunes, but I stayed right next to the water and had no problem keeping out of their way.

I reached Sand Lake around noon, near low tide. With the tide out, the lake was small, not much more than a few channels of water in the sand. Before fording the channels I had lunch, hoping the water would drop a little more. After lunch I left the beach and walked inland, possibly a quarter of a mile, to find a spot shallow enough to cross what was left of the lake. I debated with myself as to whether I should leave my shoes on to protect the raw exposed end of my little toe or to take them off so I'd have dry shoes for my feet later. I decided to take them off and waded across the channel to an island and then across another channel. When I was putting my shoes back on I discovered a blister on the little toe of my right foot that matched the blister on my left foot, but about a day behind it in condition. It hadn't torn away from the toe like the left one had. I suspect it probably will.

After wiping most of the sand off my feet and putting my shoes on I hiked back toward the beach, where I encountered another channel I had to cross. It was more of a hassle than it was worth to get all the sand off my feet to put my shoes back on, so I just left them on this time and waded across. After about an hour of this, I had crossed Sand Lake and returned to the beach. The next landmark was Cape Kiwanda, about four more miles south.

Looking for a place shallow enough to wade across.
This is covered with water at high tide.

I had taken the legs off of my pants earlier in the day when I got hot climbing the north side of Cape Lookout. I should have put sunscreen on as soon as I reached the beach, but I waited until I was almost to Cape Kiwanda and by then it was too late. I got a bit of a burn but I don't think it's too bad. I'll find out tonight or tomorrow.

South side of Cape Kiwanda. I walked over the huge sand dune on the right.

The climb over Cape Kiwanda was unlike any other cape or head yet. It was just an oversized sand dune. I used my trekking poles in the soft sand and they helped me push my way to the top.

I came down the other side and walked the beach a short distance to the little town of Cape Kiwanda. A map at the visitor information station guided me back to the beach for a short walk south to the access to Pacific City and on to Pacific City Inn, where Dionne had made reservations for Friday and Saturday nights. I arrived at the motel at about 3:45 p.m. and got to work cleaning and sorting my gear and writing in my journal. Dionne arrived at about 6:30 and we went out for dinner.

Day 7
Saturday, June 23
Rest Day

No hiking today. It is a rest day for my feet and they really need it. I wore sandals all day so my feet would get a lot of air. They're feeling pretty good now but they'll get a pretty good beating again tomorrow.

This morning we drove up to Oceanside so I could share the enchantment of that little town with Dionne, but when we arrived it started raining. Since neither of us was dressed for rain, we watched the ocean through the car window and took a nap. After a while we decided to drive to Newport and check out the art galleries.

On the way to Newport we did something we have never done: we picked up a hitchhiker. He was a young man, about 20 years old, carrying a high tech carbon fiber skateboard and a backpack up a long hill. I pulled over and asked him where he was going and at first he just said, "Over the top of this hill," then added that he was skateboarding to San Luis Obispo, CA. I invited him into the car and he filled us in on what he was doing. When he gets to a hill that is too steep to skate up, or down, he hitchhikes. He says about 20% of the trip from Olympia has been in cars. I've never met a skateboard traveler and we pummeled him with questions, which he was happy to answer. He in turn asked me questions about my pack and equipment because my pack weight is only twenty-four pounds and his is forty. We let him out way before my curiosity was satisfied.

In Newport, Dionne and I had lunch at Mo's and then went to our favorite art gallery. While we were there an artist delivered a bronze cast singing bowl. It was about 12 inches in diameter and as the rim is rubbed in a circular motion with a wood dowel, it comes to life with a deep hum. We were taken by it and thought it would fascinate the grandkids, so we bought it.

Singing bowl.

We were in Newport only a couple of hours, then returned to Pacific City for dinner and to finish preparations for tomorrow. I'm always surprised at how busy I stay organizing equipment and planning and writing in my journal.

My son, Chris, will be joining me on the hike tomorrow. He wasn't able to get a ride to the coast, so tomorrow morning I'll leave Dionne here in Pacific City to enjoy the beach and I'll drive the 75 miles to Corvallis to bring Chris back here to walk with me for a few days.

My week of being alone is completed. I have traveled 120 miles of beaches, roads and trails, and, other than the blisters on my toes and sunburn on my legs, I've fared pretty well. The scenery has been fantastic. I've traveled on roads less than I expected to and experienced the coast as no driver or biker ever could. I went two days without seeing anyone else on the trail, other than at parks and towns. I've had some discomfort and a little anxiety, partly from getting out of my comfort zone and partly, I think, from sleep deprivation. But I've enjoyed a much greater measure of pleasure than pain while walking the trails and beaches and experiencing the environment while I contemplate life and the new freedom I have to enjoy it.

After completing the coast hike and looking back on these early days of roller coaster emotions I have come to the conclusion that it wasn't just a lack of sleep or food or sunshine that put me in a funk. It was mostly being alone. I was alone for the first week of the hike and that is the only time I had to deal with the funk. After the first few days I adapted and the funks became fewer, but when I was joined by my son Chris or Michael or Charlie or Dionne or my sister Karen, I was never in a funk. (Maybe a bad mood once in a while, but never a funk.) I guess I'm not used to being alone.

FOUR DAYS WITH CHRIS

Day 8
Sunday, June 24

O N Sunday morning, June 24th, I drove the 150 mile round trip from Pacific City to Corvallis to pick up my 24 year-old son, Christopher. When we got back to Pacific City, Chris and Dionne and I had a late breakfast at a local restaurant and then the journey resumed.

Breakfast with Chris and Dionne in Pacific City.

The three of us walked to the south end of the North Nestucca Spit. I hadn't been able to arrange a boat across the channel, so backtracking was the only option. When we got to the end of the spit, we turned around and walked about three miles back to Pacific City. Then Dionne drove us around the bay to Winema Beach, where she said goodbye.

Goodbye to Dionne.

*Seals lazing on the sand behind Chris and me
at the end of the Nestucca Bay North Spit.*

Chris and I walked north, back to the Nestucca Bay channel and directly across the water from where we had hiked on the spit earlier. Then we turned south onto Kiwanda Beach. This complied with my rule that I walk every step of the way to California.

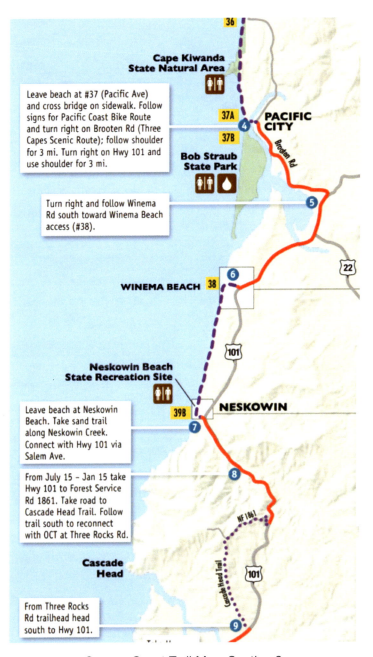

Oregon Coast Trail Map, Section 3.

View north from Porter Point at the end of the spit across Nehalem Bay, with Cape Kiwanda close and Cape Lookout in the distance.

Chris and I left Kiwanda Beach at Neskowin and had pizza for lunch at the Cafe on Hawk Creek. The next leg of the journey was a short walk on Highway 101 to the trailhead of the Cascade Head Trail. I was really looking forward to getting off the road and into the woods.

As we entered the trail, Chris saw a sign lying on the ground face down. He picked it up and read: "Trail Closed Due to Hazardous Tree Falls." We looked at each other for a moment, then he dropped it back on the ground. We pretended he hadn't picked it up and started up the trail. If I had it to do again, I wouldn't make the same decision. For two and a half miles we hiked the worst trail conditions I had ever experienced. There was a bad storm last winter and high winds had blown trees down everywhere. We climbed over, under, and around piles of downed trees. Sometimes the trail was obliterated by a pulled stump or covered beyond recognition.

Progress was slow but we eventually made it to the ridge. We were pleased to find that trees had not been knocked down on the south side of the head. I was really glad to have Chris with me on this portion of the hike. With two of us traveling together, we were able to hand our packs across logs to each other. Another set of eyes and legs to scout out alternate routes and find lost sections of the trail was also a big help. There was some stress in not knowing if we would reach a point where we just could not go any further and would have to turn back. It was comforting to not be alone in these conditions.

Chris trying to figure out how to get through a pile of downed trees.

We hiked a short distance down the south side of Cascade Head and found the problem of downed trees had been replaced with berry bushes that had grown over the trail. Since the trail was officially closed, even the good parts hadn't been maintained or used enough to clear the brush. We had to push through and duck under an almost continuous wall of berry branches. About a quarter of a mile down the south side I noticed that the new pedometer Dionne brought to me was no longer on my belt, so I left my pack with Chris and made my way back to the ridge where I'd last used it. Unfortunately, the foliage was just too dense and I was not able to find it. It was getting late in the evening so we traveled only about a mile below the ridge, where we stopped to set up camp at 8:30 in a clearing a short distance from the trail. We hadn't traveled far from where I had last used the pedometer so I was able to make a reasonable estimate of the day's journey at about 17 miles. We had bread and jam and dried apples for dinner and went to bed. I continue to be surprised at how little food I seem to need on the trail. I never would have thought that a piece of bread would satisfy me after a long day of hiking.

Day 9
Monday, June 25

I had hoped that camping away from the ocean would be warmer and drier. It wasn't. I had a very cold and fitful sleep while listening to rain falling on the hammock cover. We managed to sleep in relatively late in the morning and didn't get out on the trail until after 7:00. Chris said the quilt and pad I made had kept him warm. I suggested we trade. I pointed out all the character he would develop if he suffered the cold nights in my tiny one-pound sleeping bag instead of that nice warm quilt. He wasn't interested in building character.

The sky was blue and we were all set for a pleasant, sunny, dry walk out of the woods. That was not to be. The berry bushes became thicker as we dropped elevation. In some places they were almost impenetrable. Chris and I took turns taking the lead to push through the brush. To make things worse, the leaves were covered with water from the previous night's rain. In a short time we were soaked through. It was worse than walking on a clear path in the rain. I don't know how it penetrated my rain jacket but at one point I felt sloshing water in the arm of my jacket. I pulled at the wrist elastic and water actually poured out of the jacket sleeve.

Chris on the Not-A-Trail going down the south side of Cascade Head.

I was never so happy to break out of the woods and get onto a road as when we got off that trail. We wrung out our clothes and put them back on to dry while we walked in the sunshine toward Lincoln City.

A lady in a van drove up as we left the trailhead. We got to talking and I told her that we had just come over Cascade Head on the Oregon Coast Trail. "Oh that's nice," she said, "I just dropped my husband off on the other side of the head and he's riding the Coast Trail on his bike." I said, "You don't mean around the head?" "No," she said, "Over the head." I said, "He can't do it on a bike. There are windfalls and the trail is blocked. We were barely able to do it on foot." "He's very strong," she added, "he can do it." "How long ago did you drop him off?" "About 45 minutes ago," she said. "He should be showing up soon." I pointed at the trail and said, "There is no way he can make it over the head on that trail with a bike."

She finally understood that we were talking about different things. "Oh, not on the trail, on the road." Between the two of us, we were confusing the terms Oregon Coast Trail and Oregon Coast Bike Route. She had Chris and me thoroughly convinced that her husband was trying to ride his bike on the trail and it was a relief to understand that he was riding on the road. As we were leaving she offered us a lift through Lincoln City. We thanked her but declined, saying we were walking the entire distance to California.

I have never been impressed with Lincoln City. It seems like a long strip mall that happens to be located at the beach, but today I was happy to see it. We were almost dry from walking about four miles in the sunshine on Highway 101, but my feet were hurting and we were hungry and ready for a break. Though it was lunchtime, we had a big breakfast of pancakes, eggs and bacon in Lincoln City at the Pig-n-Pancake. After breakfast/lunch I sat on a curb and treated my blisters. The next stop was Bi-Mart, where I found a pedometer to replace the one I'd lost and I also picked up an aluminized sun blocker like those used in car windshields to insulate against the sun. I thought it would make a fine insulated pad for the bottom of my hammock.

We were able to get on the beach at the north end of Lincoln City, so we had a great ocean view rather than the strip mall view. When we reached the "D" River (claimed to be the shortest river in the world), I called Devils Lake State Park, which was just a few blocks away, to see if they had any yurts available. My right foot was hurting badly and I wanted to get off of it for the day and have a nice warm place to stay and dry out our equipment. There were no yurts available, so we decided to continue walking on the beach parallel to Lincoln City until we reached the south end of town at the Siletz Bay channel.

South end of Lincoln City and no fisherman to take us across the bay . . .

It took all afternoon to travel the length of Lincoln City. There were no fishermen to take us across Siletz Bay and we were hungry, so we walked east toward Highway 101 and had a meal at Mo's. We walked on the highway around Siletz Bay and got back on the beach at Gleneden Beach and walked south to Lincoln Beach.

. . . so we walked the road to Gleneden Beach.

As we came off the south end of Lincoln Beach at 7:30 p.m., we walked right by a family reunion and were invited to join them for dinner, which we gladly accepted. It had been three hours since we'd eaten at Mo's in Lincoln City.

Invitation to dinner at a family reunion.

At this point it was getting late and we needed to find a place to stay. Chris noticed a logging operation on the east side of Highway 101 and we found a fine site to stealth camp right near the highway. The trees were perfect for hanging the hammocks. We traveled 21.5 miles today. My total mileage was up to 158.5 miles.

9:00 p.m. and ready for bed. (He's young and needs to get to bed early.)

Day 10
Tuesday, June 26

I slept better last night. The windshield reflector really helped keep the cold from coming up through the bottom of the hammock. I still got cold but not nearly as bad.

I expected the logging operation to start early so I set my alarm for 5:00 so we could get packed and out of there before we had company. We actually got up at 4:45. Even at that, there were logging trucks entering the area before we got packed and out at 5:25 a.m.

We had to walk quite a few miles on the road today but the scenery was nice. We took a long break in Depot Bay. I took my shoes off and watched the Coast Guard practice towing boats into the "World's Smallest Harbor" while Chris took a nap. It was a great time for a break. It was early in the day but the sun was warming us, there was no wind, and we'd found a nice grassy spot at the end of a road just south of the entrance to the bay.

Coast Guard boat leaving Depot Bay Channel.

We relaxed there for an hour and a half before getting back on the road. The road walk improved immensely when we turned off of Highway 101 and got on Otter Crest Loop. A good portion of the loop has one lane of lightly traveled southbound traffic and one bike lane. It was a pleasant walk and we had great views of the rocky shoreline.

Walking the Otter Crest Loop.

From Otter Crest Loop we walked on Highway 101 to Devil's Punchbowl. After twelve miles of walking we stopped for lunch at another Mo's. They seem to be everywhere. Other than a short stretch of road walking around Yaquina Head, we had a nice long walk on the beach all the way to the south end of Newport. The weather continued to be perfect, with a light breeze coming off the ocean and blue sky above.

Looking down at Devil's Punch Bowl, Yaquina Head Lighthouse in the distance.

This was a hard day for me. The multiple blisters on my right foot were a constant annoyance. The regular routine at every rest stop was to replace the blister pads and band-aids that were falling off, take a couple of ibuprofen tablets and then hobble for about fifteen minutes until the medicine and repetition dulled the pain and I could walk at an almost normal gait again.

Chris was having some trouble too. His knees were hurting, aggravated by old marching band injuries. He was taking ibuprofen too. All that and it was still a joy to have nothing more important to do than hike along the ocean shore, smelling the fresh salt air, dodging an occasional high wave, enjoying the view, and having intermittent conversations with Chris. The pleasure was greater than the pain. When we reached the south end of Newport we had walked 23 miles and I was happy to pay the money to check into a motel and get off my feet for a while.

We cleaned ourselves up and opened up our gear to air out in the motel room, then hiked the short distance into old town Newport to find dinner. I was hoping we could spend some time in the galleries so I could show Chris a "singing bowl" like the one Dionne and I bought last weekend, but by the time Chris and I got there at a little after 6:00 p.m. on a Tuesday, all the galleries were closed. We did have a good meal though.

Day 11
Wednesday, June 27

Wednesday morning greeted us with a few high clouds and great walking conditions. Unfortunately my right foot was worse. I took the liner out of my shoe to see if that would help but it didn't. I just hobbled along until the ibuprofen dulled the pain to the point that I could ignore it. After walking across the Yaquina Bay Bridge we got back on the beach and walked along the water's edge all morning. The conditions were perfect. The sand was firm, which made for easy walking, there was no breeze, the sun was warm but not hot, my feet had become numb to the pain, and Chris's knees were feeling good. We took our shoes off to cross a creek and it felt so good to be barefoot that we carried our shoes for about half a mile before putting them back on.

At Seal Rock my guide book says you can hike the beach to Seal Rock, but it doesn't tell you how to get over or around it. I continue to be challenged by the guide book I'm using for this trip. It leaves out a lot of important details about just where the transitions are from beach to trail to road. On the other hand, the book has been a valuable resource and I wouldn't have wanted to be without it.

Dead end (almost) at Seal Rock.

I searched the area for quite a while before finding what appeared to be a private beach access trail. There were no "Keep Out" signs so we took our chances. Fortunately we didn't end up in someone's backyard. The trail delivered us to a private driveway, about twenty feet from the highway.

Chris approaching the trail off the beach.

We walked on the highway to Seal Rock State Wayside and took a nice long break. After a short walk on the road we got back on the beach south of Seal Rock. We had been walking on the beach for a while when we came upon a large flock of seagulls. Chris said he had an urge to run through the flock but he didn't make a move to do it. I said, "Why not?" So he took off his pack and dashed out into the middle of the flock like a little kid, waving his arms as he went.

Kids!

Looking north to Yaquina Head Lighthouse (where we were 22 hours ago).

We continued to enjoy walking on the sandy shoreline as we proceeded to Waldport, but we stayed on the beach a little too long and traveled too far south on the spit. When we crossed to the east side of the spit, we found we had to walk back north to get to the Alsea Bay Bridge. We crossed the bridge and arrived at the south end of Waldport at 5:30 after walking 20 miles for the day. In the four days that Chris was with me we traveled 80 miles from Pacific City. It was great to have him with me for four days and I was sorry that his part of the trip was over. We waited for Chris's friend Trenton to give us a ride to Corvallis.

Wednesday, June 27th and the end of the hike for Chris.

When Trenton arrived we all had fish and chips at Waldport Seafood Company before driving to Corvallis. He dropped us off at Chris's place, where I waited a few minutes for Dionne to arrive and take me back home to Tigard for some rest and much needed recovery time for my feet.

I spent the time at home taking care of some chores and preparing my gear for the next phase of the trip with two of my running partners, Michael and Charlie. Our other running partner, Tim had his priorities all messed up. Instead of joining us, he was going on a honeymoon in Costa Rica with his new bride.

TWO DAYS WITH MICHAEL AND CHARLIE

Day 12
Saturday, June 30

MICHAEL AND CHARLIE arrived at my house early Saturday morning and we all got into Charlie's car and drove to Waldport for the continuation of the hike. It had rained during my two days of rest, but when we arrived in Waldport the sky was clear and hiking conditions were perfect. The two days off had done wonders for my feet, and my pack was a couple of pounds lighter with most of the electronics, chargers, palm, and keyboard in the resupply box and only two days of provisions in my pack. Our tummies were full after a good breakfast at the Sea Dog Bakery and Cafe in Waldport, and after a very short walk on the road, we were at the water's edge with a nice long hike on the beach ahead of us, walking toward Yachats and Cape Perpetua.

The walk to Yachats is fantastic. The sand is firm and easy to walk on, the views are great, there is a slight breeze, and the temperature is just right. As we approach Yachats, there are rocky areas on the beach to add a little variety to the view and terrain. After eight miles of beach walking we arrive at the Yachats 804 Trail that takes us along a rocky beach with continuous viewpoints.

Almost to Yachats.

On the 804 Trail into Yachats with Charlie and Michael.

Rocks are hard to walk on!

View along the 804 Trail.

We follow a back road, Ocean View Drive, from the 804 Trail into Yachats. Marvin, "The Sun Dragon," sells us cherries and tells us stories, and he recommends The Drift Inn for lunch.

Hiking advice and cherries from Marvin, "The Sun Dragon."

After a short walk on 101 out of Yachats, we leave the highway and take the Amanda Trail to the top of Cape Perpetua. The trail is lush with trees and bushes and a nice change from the beach. There is sunlight flowing through the trees along the trail and once in a while we get a nice view of the ocean below and to the north. I'm pleased that Michael and Charlie are enjoying some of the best hiking conditions I've experienced on the Oregon Coast Trail. Again, my maps are not the best and after three miles of hiking we come to an intersection in the trail and we aren't quite sure which way to go. I take a chance on a left turn and soon find a road, but again we are not sure which way to go on it. We decide to go up the road to a day use area and see if there is an area map. We get lucky and find we've arrived at the top of Cape Perpetua and the trail south starts right at the sign where we are standing.

*Finding our way off of Cape Perpetua (they should have hired a better guide)
at 5:00 p.m. and 15 miles.*

The trail down the south side of Cape Perpetua is very picturesque with great views to the south. We have a four-mile trail walk down off of Cape Perpetua which includes a stop at the Cape Perpetua Visitor Center for a short break.

Looking south from Cape Perpetua. Heceta Head is in the distance, where we will be tomorrow morning.

As soon as we come off the Cape there is no longer a trail or beach we can walk on. That puts us back on the shoulder of Highway 101 for a seemingly endless eight-mile walk to Carl G. Washburne Memorial State Park, where we will camp. (What would take about ten minutes by car takes about three hours of walking.)

The ideal conditions we've had all day are behind us. The weather and the views continue to be great but the continuous highway walking begins to get on our nerves, plus the fact that we aren't really sure how far it is to a place to camp. Carl G. Washburne is a long way away and we are hoping to find a good place that's closer. When you want to find a place to camp but can't and you have to continue for miles with cars and trucks whizzing by it becomes very tiring. At 26.2 miles I point out to Michael and Charlie that we have completed a marathon, but Michael is not impressed with an eleven-hour marathon. Having found no place to camp earlier, we finally arrive at Carl G. Washburne at 9:00 p.m. At 27 miles the three of us are at about the end of our energy reserves. We have a quick bite to eat, then set up camp and get into our sleeping bags.

Day 13
Sunday, July 1

Sunday morning we wake up refreshed and have breakfast, break camp, and are on our way to the beach. There will be relatively little road walking today. A short beach hike takes us to the Hobbit Trail, which goes up and over Heceta Head.

Heceta Head Lighthouse.

We are 3.5 miles from camp when we reach the lighthouse at Heceta Head. We are actually looking down at the top of the lighthouse when we pass by. The beauty of the beach and trail are quickly making up for the drudgery of yesterday evening's eight miles of road walking. The view from Heceta Head to the south includes the bridge across Cape Creek and the cliff on which the Sea Lion Caves are located. We'll have to walk the road from Heceta Head, through a tunnel and over Sea Lion Point to the beach south of Cox Rock. The views make up for the road walking, but the tunnel is a little scary. There is no walkway or shoulder in the tunnel. We have to walk on the road. Michael chooses the southbound lane. I push the "Bikes On Roadway" flashing light button at the entrance and we hotfoot it through the tunnel. We get lucky, as quite a few cars pass by in the northbound lane but only one passes us in the southbound lane. Since there is no oncoming traffic he gives us plenty of room. It is a relief when we reach the other end of the tunnel.

Surviving the tunnel at Heceta Head.

At a viewpoint just past the Sea Lion Caves we could see north to Heceta Head Lighthouse, and south all the way to the jetty at Florence, about eight miles away and our goal for the day.

View south from Sea Lion Point with Cox Rock on the left and the beach to the jetty at Florence.

It was a short walk on the road down to the beach access and soon we are on the beach. It's 10:00 a.m. and we take a break for snacks and sunscreen. The walk from here to the North Jetty of the Siuslaw River takes about three hours, all on the beach. It's an easy walk and we're feeling good. I did stop once to treat a blister but my feet aren't hurting much. We have walked 14.6 miles from camp when we reach the jetty, and then walk the road on the way to Florence. Michael and Charlie were under the impression that Florence was right at the jetty, and if you are in a car it is, but not when you are walking. As we continued to walk on the road, the troops were getting weary and looking either for Florence or a rescue. At 2:00, after about 2.5 miles and one hour of road walking, Dionne arrived from Portland with the car. This was the end of the road for Michael and Charlie. We drove them back to Waldport where their car was parked and we all had dinner together. After dinner, they went home to Portland and Dionne and I drove back to Florence.

Michael, me, and Charlie . . . and we are still friends!

After dropping off Michael and Charlie, Dionne took me back to where she had picked us up, just north of Florence. I walked the last three miles into Florence while she looked for a place to stay. She was also making and receiving lots of calls about her mother, who had been having health problems. Her family was all in agreement that we should continue the walk and they would be in touch if her mother's condition deteriorated.

My walk into Florence was relaxing. I picked some wild roses for Dionne and enjoyed the evening walk. At 6:00 and 20 miles for the day, I arrived at the harbor in the old town area of Florence. I took my pack off, sat down on a bench and enjoyed the beautiful weather and view of the harbor while I waited for Dionne. It is such a great feeling not to be in any sort of rush. Waiting is a good excuse to do nothing but enjoy the moment and this was a great place to enjoy it. But not everything was going well. When Dionne picked me up she said that the news from her family was not good. Her mother was definitely failing and though it was impossible to know when it would happen, death was likely to be near. At this point she felt that I should continue the walk and that she should drive back to Portland and get a flight to Utah to help care for her mother.

FOUR DAYS WITH DIONNE

Day 14
Monday, July 2

W**E WOKE UP** Monday morning to beautiful hiking conditions but our plans were still in flux. Dionne talked with her family this morning and we're waiting for the latest information from her mother's doctor before we part ways. We have breakfast in a nearby restaurant.

Her sister and father have told her that we should both continue the walk. This is very hard on Dionne. She wants to be with her family and help with her mother, but they say the situation is under control. Her mother could be in this condition for weeks and it would be best if she goes on the walk and stays in touch. She decides to walk.

We make arrangements with the motel manager to leave our car, and at 9:00 a.m. we start walking south toward the old town area of Florence. It is a short walk on the road to get over the Siuslaw River and back to the beach. Dionne is getting over the turmoil of all the phone calls and decisions. I'm glad I'm not walking without her.

There are no services between Florence and Winchester Bay, where we expect to be tomorrow afternoon, so our packs are heavy with extra food and water. When we got off the road and began walking on the beach, Dionne had a "this-is-why-we-do-this" moment." Those moments come every once in a while on our adventures. It happens when everything comes together just the way we had dreamed it would be. The sky was blue and there was a light breeze, but the air was warm and the sand was firm and easy to walk on. The cares of everyday life fell away. For her, the adventure had just begun.

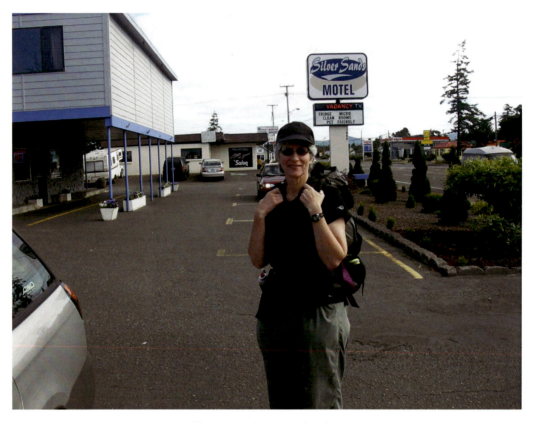

Dionne's adventure begins.

By noon we had traveled about 8 miles on this long stretch of beach. Between Florence and Winchester Bay there are no detours off the beach. The trail is on the beach all the way and we are loving it. It will be like this all day today and a good portion of tomorrow. The only thing less than perfect is that some of the beach is open to four-wheelers. The tide was coming in so the beach was narrow, making it difficult to stay out of the surf and clear of the riders. Just before we reached the end of the four-wheeler area, a man and his sons stopped to talk with us and we made the mistake of turning our gaze away from the ocean. A sneaker wave lived up to its name and soaked our shoes.

At about 2:00 and 11 miles, we arrive at the mouth of the Siltcoos River, which is too deep to ford due to the high tide. We have to walk back north to find a way off the beach to look for a bridge over the river.

At 11 miles our way is blocked by the Siltcoos River. We have to backtrack.

About an hour later we find a bridge at the Wax Myrtle campground and decide it is time for some food and a nap. It's a lovely little camp with lots of vegetation, which gives each camping spot plenty of privacy. This would be a nice place to come back to someday if we're car camping in the area.

Earlier in the day we thought we might be able to make it to Winchester Bay today, but as we leave this campground at 4:00 p.m. it is obvious that we won't. It took us 2.5 hours to get to the south side of the Siltcoos River. The day continues to be gorgeous with nothing but blue sky overhead, and we're in no hurry. At 5:00 we've traveled 16 miles and Dionne is getting pretty tired, so we slow down to an easy mosey and she is doing fine at that pace. It's nice to relax and enjoy the moment with no care for how far we go or where we'll stop for the night.

As the evening wears on we have traveled 19 miles. The clouds have come in but they're not threatening and there's a light breeze of cool air coming off the ocean. Dionne is getting a second wind and our pace has increased. We pass by a snowy plover restriction area and have to get beyond it to find a place to camp. At 7:00 we have traveled 20 miles and we find a place just off the beach behind a small dune that will block the ocean breeze.

Camping on the beach south of Siltcoos.

Our tarp tent is set up facing the northwest and we have a million dollar view of the ocean as the sun sets. We have it all to ourselves; we haven't seen anyone for hours. We get all settled in and try to stay awake to see the sunset.

View of the sunset from our tarp tent on the beach.

Day 15
Tuesday, July 3

It was a beautiful moonlit night last night and this morning the sky is clear. There is dew all over the grass, the ground, and our tent. We stayed nice and warm in our 16-ounce sleeping bags. At 6:40 we have broken camp, and I don't want to set my pack back down on the ground because sand will stick to the moisture on it and it will be a mess, so I hang it on the front of Dionne. It looks good there, but she says I have to take it back.

This is why you take your wife backpacking with you.

This will be an interesting day because we'll be walking south on a long peninsula that comes to an end at the Umpqua River and we have no idea how we'll get across to Winchester Bay and then to points south. At 10:00 and 7 miles from camp I climbed up a sand dune and was able to get cell reception. I called the harbormaster at Winchester Bay to ask him if there was anyone who would be willing to ferry a couple of hikers across the river. The cell phone reception wasn't very good and at first he thought it was a distress call and that we were out in the ocean. He was about to call the Coast Guard. I was able to explain that we were hiking the Oregon Coast Trail and just needed a boat to pick us up at the North Jetty. With that, he said he would look into it and call me back in half an hour.

Half an hour later the harbormaster, Jeff, called with good news. He said he had a friend, also Jeff, who was camping on the north shore of the Umpqua River. To get to Jeff's campsite we'd need to cross the peninsula that is bordered by the Pacific Ocean and the Umpqua River. However, Harbormaster Jeff said there is no way to get across the peninsula. We'll have to walk all the way to the south end on the beach and then head inland along the north shore of the Umpqua River. He said that if we didn't find Jeff we could call the Coast Guard. I again said that we were not in an emergency situation but he said that wasn't a problem. He had already called the Coast Guard and when he told them we were walking the Oregon Coast Trail they said they would be happy to launch an inflatable and come get us. One way or another, we would make it across. I almost hoped Jeff wouldn't be there. How exciting to be rescued by the Coast Guard!

At 11:30 and 10.5 miles we made it to the end of the jetty and headed north along the Umpqua on a number of confusing trails, many coming to dead ends in trees or driftwood.

We eventually worked our way north and found the camp and a man standing by a boat. When he saw us his first words were, "Are you lost?" I said, "If you're Jeff, I'm not lost." He gave us a puzzled look and I could tell he was trying to figure out if he knew us from somewhere. I told him that the harbormaster had told us about him and that he might be able to help us across the river. We were instantly welcomed to his camp and he introduced us to his wife, who offered us a drink and a chair. We told them our story and soon we were in his boat and on our way across the river to Winchester Bay.

No more trail.

I think one of my favorite things about our little adventures is the opportunity to be a little vulnerable and meet people who are more than happy to lend a hand. We met two of those people today, Jeff the harbormaster and Jeff the camper.

Launching Jeff's boat for our ride across the Umpqua River.

At 1:00 we were making good use of our stop in Winchester Bay. Dionne treated her first blister, and we had a nice lunch/dinner at Griff's on the Bay. After our meal, I got all of our camping equipment spread out to dry while Dionne made numerous calls to her family to find out how her mother was doing. We packed extra water, 50 ounces for each of us, for the next long trek on the beach with no services expected until tomorrow afternoon. At 4:00 we left town and were soon on the beach walking south. It wasn't long until I had another blister. I had enjoyed a couple of days with no foot pain so this was a little disappointing, but it was nothing compared to the early days of the hike.

I was amazed at how far we were able to travel again today. We had a little tailwind and the skies remained clear. At 8:00 p.m. and 23 miles, about 8 miles south of Winchester Bay, we set up our tent on the beach and settled in for the evening. The breeze was pretty stiff and we had no friendly dune for a windbreak this evening, so we sat in our tent to eat our dinner of cold oatmeal and chocolate-covered raisins.

Day 16
July 4, Independence Day

We take our time breaking camp this morning while we wait for the tide to go out enough to allow us to cross Ten Mile Creek, a little south of us. The sky was clear when we got up but it is now overcast and there is a slight breeze. Today is another day of miles of beach hiking.

There are some seals just off shore watching us and even moving a little south with us as we walk. We will not be so adventurous today; we will not walk down the peninsula to the mouth of Coos Bay. We have no known way to get across, and also we'll have missed any chance of a meal and a place to stay in North Bend if we do get across. The plan is to walk to Horse Fall Beach and then leave the beach and walk the road over the McCullough Bridge into the town of Coos Bay.

As we walk the beach I think about art projects I want to do, and once in a while we stop and I sketch my ideas in the sand to explain them to Dionne. We talk about life, our families, our hopes and dreams, but most of the time we don't talk. We observe, listen, and feel.

Crossing Ten Mile Creek.

Kinetic art idea.

We left the beach after maybe 10 miles of hiking. From Horse Fall Park we have about a seven-mile road walk to North Bend. A short distance from the beach we lost the cool ocean breeze and found ourselves shedding a layer of clothes. We walked by a sawmill that I visited about six months ago when I was still working for Weyerhaeuser. My engineering group toured several sawmills to look at equipment for possible use in a new mill in Longview, Washington. At the time I was already planning this trip and as the group of us toured mills along the coast, I was watching for landmarks and scouting routes, and dreaming of what I would be doing in a few months. And now I am doing it and loving it!

McCullough Bridge across Coos Bay.

At a little after 1:00 p.m. we were on a causeway headed for the McCullough Bridge. The wind was stronger than anything we had experienced before on this trip and it got even stronger as we hiked across the bridge, high above the water. We held on to the handrails to keep wind gusts from blowing us off the walkway and into the road. I'm glad it wasn't so windy in 2001 when we walked our bikes across this bridge. At 2:30 and 17 miles we were across the bridge and resting in a little park. I'm afraid that park was the last nice place we saw until we left North Bend. North Bend is not much to look at and there is plenty of it, but we found a good place to eat and checked into a motel at about 7:30, having hiked 21 miles that day.

Day 17
Thursday, July 5

Dionne is still struggling with whether to continue the hike or take a bus or taxi and head back to the car in Florence. She calls her family and again decides to carry on. Today will be all road walking, following pretty much the same route that we took when we rode our bikes to California in 2001. The scenery didn't improve much until 10:00 when we had walked 8 miles to the little fishing town of Charleston, but the weather was good and we had a nice wide paved sidewalk most of the way.

Charleston was a breath of fresh air. We stopped there for snacks and rest and collected information from a very helpful fellow at the visitor information center. He found a bus route schedule and brought it to us at the little store we had stopped at to get a snack. (I had a donut and a pint of chocolate milk and I'm still losing weight.) At 10:45 we were on our way out of town, knowing we were anywhere from 18 to 30 miles away from Bandon, depending on which of the locals we chose to believe. We soon found a sign saying it is 24 miles to Bandon, so about an average of the two is close.

We continue to walk on the roads but there is very little traffic, especially when we get through Charleston and on to Seven Devils Road. As I walk I'm thinking about the art I intend to create when I settle into my new life as an artist. I've tried portrait art and murals but what I really enjoy is kinetic sculpture. I have lots of things I want to try in that medium. I wonder what the future will bring. Will I be a successful artist or will I go some other way with my life? This hike is just the first adventure in my new life as a retiree. My mind comes back to the present as we pass a number of tired old homesteads on this route. There are many signs of lost dreams along the road, old rusted out buses, recreational vehicles, boats, equipment and houses that are falling apart, probably a result of the downturn in the timber industry, which used to be very strong in this area but has now almost disappeared.

Impoverished neighborhood with lots of dead cars, RVs, and junk.

At 2:00 p.m. we have walked 15 miles and it's another 17 miles to Bandon. If we make it, that will be a huge hiking day. Dionne is getting tired and has sore feet but feels that she can go another 10 miles. I am starting to look for places off the side of the road where we can set up a stealth camp for the night but she feels like continuing. We will find a place when she feels like stopping.

I've been looking at my maps and at the mile markers and I am in one of those situations where I know which way I should continue to go but I don't really know where I am. Is that considered being lost or just a little confused? I have no question that we should be continuing in the same direction on this road and that we will make it to Bandon if we stay on this road. But I think we missed a turn a few miles back and I don't think this is the road I intended to be on. If so, it only means we will be getting to the same place at the same distance, just not on the route we expected.

At 5:00 and 21 miles, we find ourselves at the intersection of Whiskey Lane and Beaver Hill Road about ten miles north of Bandon. This is also the end of the road for us. Dionne just got cell coverage and called her sister and found that her mother has taken a turn for the worse. We were fortunate that we were on roads rather than beaches today. We will be able to get a cab to pick us up on this road. A wave of disappointment flowed through me as I ended the hike by calling a taxi. But it wasn't like this was an epic journey, just a hike down the coast. I'd get over it. I called Karen, my sister, who was about to leave Post Falls, Idaho and meet us in Bandon to walk the rest of the way to California with us. She was disappointed but understood. Within fifteen minutes of the call, a taxi picked us up and we were on our way back to Florence, 80 miles north by road. (What took us four days to walk will take about an hour and a half by car. I can see why walking has gone out of style as a means of travel.)

Hike interrupted after 16 hiking days and 332 miles.

He was paid well for the 80-mile trip.

ON THE ROAD AGAIN
WITH KAREN

Day 18

Sunday, August 5

A LOT HAS HAPPENED since we left the hike a month ago. There has been a funeral for Dionne's mom, a wedding for my oldest son, Levi, and a 60th wedding anniversary for my folks. Karen, my sister, has joined the adventure. Dionne was not able to make it for this portion (someone has to work) but she will join us in a few days. Karen dropped me off at the same spot where the cab driver picked Dionne and me up a month ago, and then she drove to Bandon.

The hike resumes at the intersection of Whiskey Lane and Beaver Hill Road.

I'm running the ten miles to Bandon with a light day pack. It was another beautiful day and it wasn't long until the euphoria of being back on the hike kicked in. I arrived in Bandon in 1 hour and 40 minutes. I gave Karen the option of staying the night in Bandon or starting the walk south. She had butterflies about the hike and thought she was more likely to feel better if we got started. So we had a good meal, picked up a few supplies and left town at 4:30 p.m.

Karen is ready for the Big Adventure.

My car is parked (with permission) at the visitor center. We put our packs on, 22 pounds each, fully loaded with all of our gear and food and water, and we are on our way!

5:20 p.m. and Karen is happy to be here.

A few miles down the beach, the tide almost blocked our way but by timing the waves and running we got to the next section of beach with dry feet.

Timing the waves.

Spectacular rock formations south of Bandon.

Karen found a 10-inch diameter plastic fishing float that she wanted to keep. I convinced her that adding the weight of that float to her pack would not be a good idea. (This was a tactical error on my part; not letting her lug that thing down the beach was contrary to my Plan of Revenge.) She made do with a photo of it. The sky was about 90% overcast and the sea breeze was cool. The sand was softer than what I'd been used to north of here. Even the wet sand is soft.

Karen's first float sighting.

I should introduce Karen. She is my "older" sister. When we were children, it was her job to harass her little brother and it was her little brother's job to get revenge. I didn't do a good job of the revenge stuff at the time, not being big enough or creative enough to do her much harm. Although she seems to think I did a fine job, I don't feel that I completed my assigned task, and thus I have invited her to join me on this hike. I expect there will be countless ways that nature can inflict suffering on her and I will appear to be entirely innocent. In fact, I will be considered by many to be quite kind to have invited her to join me on this adventure. So let the long-awaited revenge begin!

It is a cool overcast evening with a mild breeze off the ocean. At 8:30, after four hours of hiking, we decided to call it a day and move off of the beach a little to get some protection from the wind and pitch the tent. We located our camp on the sand in a trough between two sand dunes. We called this Guerilla Camp because the pair of big black float balls we found there looked like mines.

Guerilla Camp.

Karen and I had a miscommunication about how much water we would need and she ended up with 20 ounces less than what I'd hoped she would have. There is no water available around here and we don't expect to find any for a while tomorrow. I'm sure we will survive.

We did amazingly well today with such a late start. We are 10 miles south of Bandon and 20 miles from where Karen dropped me off this morning.

Day 19
Monday, August 6

It's surprising how soft sand is when you walk on it and how hard it is when you sleep on it. I woke up with some aches and pains this morning. Tonight I'm going to move the sand around to fit the contours of my body before I lie down on it. This morning we are packed and on our way by 6:30. There is 100% cloud cover but no wind and the sand is still soft.

We will walk on soft sand all day and see no one for hours on end in this remote area south of Bandon.

Shortly after leaving camp I find a three-inch diameter float and since I didn't let Karen keep the big one, I give her this one. Now she's a happy camper.

"Seriously, Ken?"

Since the sand is so soft, we try to walk as close to the surf as possible, but we find that the wet sand is no easier to walk on. Eventually we give up and walk higher on the beach so we don't have to keep dodging the surf. We get our trekking poles out and they help considerably.

All of my previous experience with hiking on beaches has been on the North Oregon Coast. There it is simple. Dry sand is soft and difficult to walk on and wet sand is firm and easy to walk on. Now I find out that not all sand is the same.

Maybe it has something to do with the shape or size of the sand particles. It would be interesting to know. But for whatever reason, this sand is soft, wet or dry.

We are entertained by flocks of pelicans flying north all in a row along the shore. They dip down in the wave troughs and then swoop back up as the crest comes under them.

A squadron of pelicans.

After five miles we stop for a breakfast of power bars, nuts, and dried apples. We skip the oatmeal to conserve water since we are down to 26 ounces between the two of us. There is no one else on the beach to beg for water and nowhere to resupply for a while.

At about 10:00 and maybe 8 miles from camp I see lots of footprints in the sand, so I climb up over a dune and there is the Floras Lake Campground where we can get water, just a quarter of a mile away! We aren't going to die! We divide the last 16 ounces of water and Karen gulps hers down before we walk ten steps towards the camp. My portion doesn't last much longer.

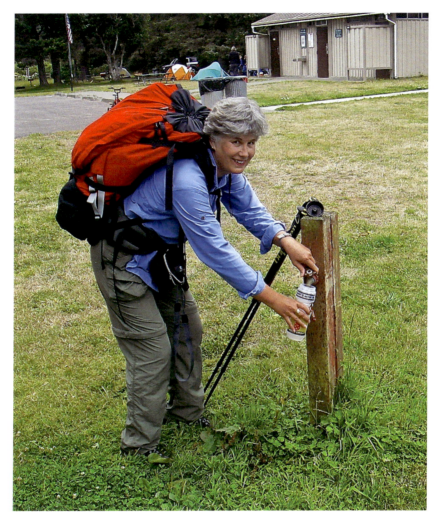

We survived!

As we entered the park we were greeted by a camper who asked us about our packs and was impressed with our journey. She gave us a bag of fresh strawberries. What a treat! We drank and ate and then with our water bottles full we headed back out to the beach on our way to the Sixes River. We had to arrive at the river sometime close to noon in order to be able to cross at low tide. We have a deadline so we are trying to walk fairly fast, but the soft sand isn't helping. (My older sister is complaining about the soft sand, my revenge is coming along well.)

Karen on soft sand.

It is impossible to get around Blacklock Point on the beach and we were fortunate to find a local who showed us the trail to hike over it. It takes us an hour and at 1:00 we arrive back on the beach.

Blacklock Point.

Karen coming down from Blacklock Point.

We race for the Sixes River, but low tide was an hour ago and we are at risk of the rising tide blocking our way. It's a shame to hurry through here because it is a very scenic area. I go ahead of Karen to find a place to ford the river and she walks in my tracks, which helps a little in the soft sand. At 1:30 I found a good place to wade through the river. The tide is coming in fast but we make it across! The next challenge is to get across the Elk River. I think we've gone about 15 miles so far today.

Karen crossing the Sixes River.

A short distance beyond the Sixes River and just north of Cape Blanko there is a magical little stream flowing over a base of multicolored rocks. It is tempting to pick up a bunch of these shiny little colored beauties and take them with us but that wouldn't be wise on a backpacking trip. I make do with a few photos.

Magical stream with shiny colored beauties.

Cape Blanco Lighthouse.

It's 3:20 when we reach the top of Cape Blanco and we know the tide will be high when we reach the Elk River. My guide book says, *"This river usually does not reach the ocean in the summer and fall so the chances are the river crossing will be dry. If it is too deep to cross safely, find the farm road on the north side of the river and follow it to the highway."* We made our way across Cape Blanco and through the campground, and with full confidence that we would get past Elk River one way or another, we descended back down to the beach and continued our hike to the river. We are looking forward to getting across it and reaching Port Orford for a much anticipated big dinner in a restaurant. We arrive at Elk River at

4:45 and the crossing does not look promising. I take my shoes off and start to wade into it, but the water is flowing too fast and too deep and it's too cold! The south shore of the river is just thirty feet away and from there it's an easy walk to Port Orford, but we can't get across.

The guide book incorrectly says we can cross the Elk River even at high tide.

Next I try to find the farm road described in my guide book. There isn't any road near the beach and there is a mountain of sand along the length of the beach. I didn't want to climb it but I didn't want to backtrack either. I told Karen to wait on the beach and I climbed up to look for the road. I got over the top of the sand and found a brush-filled ravine. I had to drop down into the ravine, climb back out, then traverse another steep mountain of sand. When I got to the top my route was blocked by a fence bordering someone's back yard and there was no way around it. The road had to be just beyond this house. I didn't want to trespass or get shot and I wasn't sure Karen could make it up here anyway, so I gave up and went back to the beach. I'd been gone so long on my scouting trip that Karen decided that she should follow my tracks up the sand. She was nearly to the top of the first cliff when I saw her. I called out and told her to go back down to the beach.

We were unable to cross the Elk River. I climb a sand cliff looking for the farm road that is referred to in the guide book.

Instead of a nice walk to Port Orford and a much anticipated meal, we walked back to Cape Blanco looking forward to power bars for dinner. The distance we covered exploring and backtracking would have gotten us to Port Orford. It left me in a bit of a bad mood. We climbed back up to the top of Cape Blanco and hiked to the campground we had passed through hours ago. We were tired and hungry after our 22 mile day and didn't have much to eat. Fortunately we were able to get a cabin and the campground had hot showers.

We had really looked forward to a real dinner in Port Orford tonight.

We put our backpacks in the cabin, had a quick bite to eat, and headed for the showers. When I first turned on the shower, I had to jump back to get away from the single solid stream of scalding hot water. The knob on the shower head was broken so I couldn't adjust it to spray. I tried to stand to the side and splash the water up on my body with my hand but it burned my hand. I crouched down low hoping the stream would be cooler at the bottom but it was still too hot. I almost gave up in despair, the final insult to a day that had ended badly at the Elk River. I was standing cold and naked by a stream of water that was too hot to touch. With one last effort, I tried pushing up on the nozzle to simulate what the adjusting knob would do if it were there. It worked! The pencil thin stream of hot water turned into a billowing mist. I stepped under it and it started to feel good, real good. I washed and rinsed and when the timer shut it off, I decided to push the button again and to just relax in the fog of heat that was enveloping me. When it shut off a couple of minutes later I pushed the button again, and then again, and again. Then it occurred to me that someone could be waiting for the shower. I checked outside and no one was waiting so I went back in and pushed the button again, and again, and again, and again, and it felt so good and I felt so good. My bad mood was washed away.

I went back to the cabin and got knocked over by an 80 degree heat wave when I opened the door. Karen had the heater going full blast to dry the clothes she had washed when she took her shower. We reached a compromise; she could continue to use the heater if I could open some windows to get some air in the place. Between my decadent shower and her clothes drying, we had a pretty big carbon footprint that evening.

I got out my maps and tide tables to figure out what we would have to do to get past the Elk River the next day. Our options were limited. Low tide would be sometime in the middle of the night and again sometime around noon tomorrow. We weren't in the mood for a night hike or for hanging around here for half a day so the only thing left was to walk the road from the campground out to Highway 101 and follow it the rest of the way to Port Orford.

Day 20
Tuesday, August 7

At 7:00 a.m. we left our cabin under an overcast sky but no wind, heading east toward Highway 101. There is virtually no traffic on this little access road and the scenery is nice. The road is near the Sixes River and we can look to the northwest and see where we crossed it yesterday afternoon. When we get to Highway 101 we turn south and walk on the shoulder of the road. It isn't long before we reach the bridge over the Elk River. At the middle of the bridge we stop and, with great pomp and circumstance, ceremonially spit in it to express our disdain for what it did to us yesterday. I know it isn't the river's fault. I know it was the ocean that raised the water level in the river and blocked our way, but just the same, we spat in it. And as Karen aptly pointed out, if the river had not been there, it wouldn't have risen with the ocean. With the ceremonial spit completed, we felt much better. It was good for us, it gave us closure. Now we can put this ugly incident behind us and dream of a good meal in Port Orford.

According to the sign at the entrance of the town, Port Orford is the oldest town site on Oregon's coast, established in 1851, exactly 100 years before the momentous occasion of my birth. (That last part wasn't on the sign.) At 10:00 and 9 miles, we arrive at the Paradise Cafe and indulge in a glorious breakfast of toast and ham and eggs and hash browns.

Happy camper for real.

We buy some supplies in Port Orford and at noon we head south expecting to walk on the beach to Humbug Mountain, but Karen does some checking around and is told by one of the locals that the beach route is blocked by a landslide and we will have to walk on the road for a while. I called Dionne, who is on her way from Portland to Brookings. She will leave the car there and take the bus north to join us for the rest of the walk to the California border.

Highway 101 to Humbug Mountain.

By 1:30 Karen and I have walked about 13 miles when we leave Highway 101 and take the Old Coast Road, which has become part of the Oregon Coast Trail. It is closed to all but service vehicles so there is no traffic. The views of the ocean and Humbug Mountain are great and as we walk we pick and enjoy ripe blackberries. I call Dionne again with some new information. She can park in Brookings tonight and take a taxi up to join us tonight for $80, or she can drive here and in the morning drive back to Brookings and take the bus north for about $10. She decides to drive here and meet us at Humbug Park. We arrive at the park at about 4:00, having hiked about 15 miles today. Dionne arrives at 7:20 and we all get in the car and drive the short distance back to Port Orford to get dinner and a motel. We were directed by a local to Griff's on the Dock for dinner. It was a great choice, not only for the good food but because it is located by the bay where a couple of whales were putting on a show. I had never been this close to whales in the wild. It was quite a treat.

Dionne arrives from Portland and we all return (by car)
to Port Orford for dinner and whale watching.

DIONNE REJOINS THE HIKE
(And We Almost Lose
Karen Twice)

Day 21
Wednesday, August 8

IN THE MORNING after another good breakfast, Dionne drops Karen and me off at Humbug Mountain Campground and then drives to Brookings. The day is beautiful with a clear blue sky and no wind. If we weren't walking on a shaded trail we would be getting hot. The trail is lush with leather fern, maidenhair fern, lady fern, sword fern, deer fern, west coast fern and others. It is a lovely little trail, a much longer distance than walking the road but well worth it. We continue on beautiful trails that climb and drop and switch back and forth and make wonderfully inefficient progress toward the California border.

At 10:15 we arrive at Humbug Mountain day-use park and take a break. When we leave here we'll be leaving the trails and walking on Highway 101 for a while. Shortly after we leave the park and four miles into today's walk, Karen's right foot slips off the edge of the asphalt and she takes a nasty fall, bruising her left leg and twisting her right ankle. After a bit she tries to stand up but has to sit right back down. Her ankle is beginning to swell and it appears that there may be some significant damage.

This doesn't look like something that will go away with a little bit of rest. We are in a difficult situation. Dionne will be getting on a bus from Brookings soon to come and join the hike but the hike appears to be coming to an end. Neither of our cell phones has a signal in this area so we can't call to tell her to drive back and not to get on the bus.

About 100 yards up the road there is a highway department vehicle parked on a wide gravel area. I take our packs and with her trekking poles, Karen is able to hobble up to the vehicle where we find some assistance. They offer us the use of their first aid kit, and best of all they lend us a cell phone that gets a weak but usable signal in this area. I call Dionne and the first thing I say is "Don't get on the bus." Fortunately the connection is good enough to carry on a conversation and I'm able to explain what happened and have her drive back to pick up Karen. Karen is a nurse and makes good use of the first aid kit to wrap her ankle and clean the wounds. She is really disappointed. She has been training and looking forward to this for months, but after just a little over three days of hiking it appears that she is done. (My plot of revenge is working too well.)

The nurse is treating her wounds.

Dionne arrives a little after noon and we work on an alternate plan. I empty the camping gear out of my pack and convert it to a day pack and continue south fast and light, trying to make up some time. Dionne takes Karen back to Port Orford to get ice for her ankle and more medical supplies. We are all wondering how things are going to work out, but at this point there isn't much we can do but take events as they come and deal with them.

I settle into the walk and try to move beyond the disappointment of the accident. The route is still on the shoulder of the road. The highway runs right along the coast with no accessible beaches or trails but there are nice views at times. At 2:00 and eight miles, I'm at the Prehistoric Gardens. I'm really thirsty and I'd like a cold drink but I'm afraid that if I go inside, Karen and Dionne might drive by and miss me. My thirst drives me in anyway and I get an ice cold Coke. Five minutes later Karen and Dionne drive by and wave; that was close timing. The good news is that Karen was driving. We have more options if she can drive. A few minutes later I find the two of them at a wide spot in the road, waiting for me with drinks and deli sandwiches.

After lunch, Karen takes the car and Dionne joins me. She has spent all day yesterday and most of today driving and I'm glad she's finally getting a chance to hike. I'm carrying my day pack with a few essentials and Dionne is carrying a water bottle, so we should be able to move pretty fast. We see a beautiful home down by the ocean with a for sale sign in front of it. Dionne asks me to buy it for her and I say I would but I don't want to spoil her. She says if I had a job I could buy it, but no, I quit my job and instead of making lots of money to buy her nice stuff, I take her for a long walk. We both laugh.

"Sorry, it isn't going to happen." (Humbug Mountain in the background.)

We have some great views and some sections where there is no view at all, but we find plenty of ripe blackberries along the road to eat.

Finding blackberries along the road.

We are walking fast. Dionne takes the lead and I have to move right along to keep up with her. At 4:30 and 14 miles we arrive at Opher Wayside and go down to the beach, where we again find soft sand. Most of the beaches south of Bandon are soft sand.

Walking on soft sand again.

Before long we reach Nesika Beach, where we move to a quiet side road. We stop at a little grocery store where we buy a quart of chocolate milk and sit at a table in front of the store to rest, drink, and soak up the sunshine. That was good.

We continue on the Old Coast Highway until it intersects Highway 101. It is 6:40 p.m. and I have walked 20 miles today. We are a few miles north of Gold Beach. Karen picks us up here and we all drive to Gold Beach and stay in another cheap motel.

The hike has changed its character. Karen thinks there is some hope for her ankle so she's going to stay with us and use the car to support our tour, and if things go well, she may be able to do some hiking again. That gives us a lot more flexibility as to where we stop and start each day, but the three of us will never be able to walk together. Karen (if she can) or Dionne will hike with me while the other takes the car. Having the car takes away some of the feel of independence and adventure, but we will never go hungry again and we will always be able to get to a motel.

Historic 1886 County Road.

Day 22
Thursday, August 9

Karen's ankle is feeling better this morning and she wants to try hiking. Dionne drops Karen and me off at the same spot where Karen had picked us up last night and we walk on the Old Coast Road toward Gold Beach. We could walk on the beach for a while but the sand is soft and the road is quiet so we opt for the road. It's another beautiful morning with sunshine, blue sky, and no wind. A light fog hangs over the Rogue River and surrounds a multitude of fishing boats.

Fishing boats on the Rogue River near Gold Beach.

Karen's ankle is feeling pretty good, so there is some possibility that she can carry a pack and we can go back to the original plan of leaving the car and hiking together. After walking five miles we arrive back at the motel, and Karen checks this out by carrying her full pack on the walk from the motel to the restaurant for breakfast.

Rogue River Bridge.

The three of us discuss our options while we load up on pancakes. The consensus is that we should continue with the relay, partly because of the risk of Karen's foot giving out under heavy use and partly because the logistics of getting us all back to the car at the end of the trip are complicated. With the car for support we will carry light or no packs and move relatively fast (but still try to be experience-oriented rather than goal-oriented). Since Karen hiked the first five miles this morning, Dionne will walk with me from Gold Beach to the top of Cape Sebastian. As we leave town we stop at an information booth to get details about the trail between here and Brookings.

The sun continues to shine but the breeze has picked up considerably. Dionne and I are walking on the beach with sand that is harder than any we've experienced south of Bandon, but only for a little while. It soon turns soft and Dionne walks behind me in my tracks to make it a little easier. At 11:40 and 10 miles into today's hike we reach the base of Cape Sebastian and find the trail to the top.

Finding the trail to Cape Sebastian.

It is circuitous and we find ourselves walking north almost as much as south. The trail is in relatively good condition but still challenging. There are trail intersections with no information posts so we have to guess which trail to take. We find occasional Oregon Coast Trail posts located where there are no intersections, so if we've made the right decision we do get to find out about it later. There is one major trail washout and beyond it there is brush growing over the trail.

The trail is washed out.

No sign of anyone going through here lately. As we proceed the vegetation on the trail gets thicker, and at one point the trail is blocked by a fallen tree. We get over the tree and start climbing a steep zigzag path. We are finding some nice views but the trail to the top of Cape Sebastian is difficult. You would quickly get frustrated if you let yourself become goal-oriented. We're not making good time on this section but it's a great place to enjoy the scenery. At 2:00 p.m. and 15 miles we find Karen and the car at the top of Cape Sebastian.

I've probably mentioned it before, but the amazing thing about most of these trails is that we're almost always alone on them. If you want to get away from crowded trails, hike the Oregon Coast Trail.

Looking north from the top of Cape Sebastian
with Humbug Mountain in the distance.

We have lunch and discuss the next section of trail. After experiencing the difficulty of the trail up the north side of Cape Sebastian, neither Karen nor Dionne is inclined to tackle the trail going down the south side of the cape and I agree. I go down the trail alone and soon find that we made the wrong decision. The trail on the south side of the cape is nothing like the north side. It is well cared for, easy to walk and very beautiful. I wish one of them could have enjoyed it with me.

We guessed wrong. The trail on the south side of Cape Sebastian is
in beautiful condition. Dionne or Karen should have been with me.

The sun is shining but the wind is getting pretty strong. Fortunately much of the trail is protected from the wind. I'm not carrying a pack so I find myself approaching a run at times and have to remind myself to slow down and enjoy the moment. About an hour after leaving the top of the Cape I'm back down on the beach and being pushed along by a strong tailwind on hard sand. At 3:15 and 18 miles I've reached the wayside where Karen and Dionne are waiting.

Looking back at Cape Sebastian.

I notice a windsurfer on the beach as I approach the wayside where Dionne and Karen are waiting.

After a short break, Karen joins me on the next leg of the trip down the beach toward Crook Point at the south end of Pistol River Park. As soon as we get back on the beach we are greeted with a 20-mile-per-hour wind. The wind stirs up the surface of the beach and creates rivers of dry sand. Most of it skims along a few inches above the ground but some flies higher. Walking conditions are challenging due to the soft sand and the back of our legs are getting blasted, but at least it's a tailwind. I wouldn't want this sand in my face.

Rivers of dry sand created by the wind.

This section of the walk is not well marked and the maps we have are not good. We do a lot of wandering around dunes between the beach and ponds and along cliffs, trying to find the best walking conditions (harder sand and a little shelter from the wind). We don't have much success and these forays add to the amount of walking. It's a real pain when we have to backtrack, as we get the wind and sand in our faces. We reach the south end of Pistol River Park and still have not been able to find the trail that will take us from the beach to the highway. I spend a fair amount of time climbing dunes, backtracking, and wandering around looking for the trail.

It's 4:30 p.m. and we are unsure of the route.

The trailhead we were looking for was washed out by a storm and I finally locate it at the top of a landslide. The trail takes us away from the beach and up through a sandy area with lots of brush and trees, and we are happy to get shelter from the wind. This is a loop trail and will not get us back to the highway, but according to the map there is a trail off of this one that will. At 6:00 we decide we must have missed it because the trail has curved around and we are now going north instead of east. I tell Karen to wait and I jog back along the trail for about half a mile looking for the missed turn, though I don't have much hope that we'll find it. We have cell reception and Karen calls Dionne to tell her that we don't really know where we are and that we will be late to our rendezvous.

The backtracking is fruitless. I could find no branching trail that goes southeast or any other trail for that matter, so I turned back to find Karen. When I find her we leave the trail and bushwhack due east to find Highway 101. The terrain is rough in this area and there's a fair amount of vegetation so bushwhacking is a challenge. (But hey! We're back in adventure mode even though we have the car! I guess we are lucky after all.) We are encouraged when we start to hear highway traffic, and at 6:50 we make it back to the road. It took us about an hour and a half to cover the half-mile distance from the beach to the road.

After bushwhacking our way to the highway, we found the trailhead.
We were unable to find the other end of it when we needed it.

We walked south to find a mile marker so we could tell Dionne where to find us. I checked my pedometer and found that I have walked over 26 miles, another marathon. As we walked on Highway 101 we found the south end of the trail that we were unable to find when we were wandering in the wilderness. The trail end is at mile marker 111, but there is no highway sign to identify this trailhead. Someday maybe I'll reverse walk this trail and find out where it intersects with the main trail.

Karen has a little problem with her trekking poles at times. I haven't been able to figure out how it happens, but every once in a while we'll be walking along and suddenly she's flat on her face in the sand with a trekking pole between her legs.

This happens once or twice a day and I've kind of gotten used to it. I tried to be helpful though. I told her, "You may want to quit falling on your face." But being an older sister, she won't listen to me. However, she's pretty resilient and gets right back up and we are on our way again. She had one of those little episodes just before we left the beach. When we made it to the highway I said to her, "Now that we're back to civilization, you may want to wipe that sand off your face." When she touched her face and felt the sand she started laughing and then I started laughing, and as we walked south on 101 it would come to her mind again every once in a while and she would start laughing again. That kept us in a good mood for the next couple of miles.

We continued walking south until 7:40 p.m. when Dionne found us at Burnt Hill Road. I have walked over 28 miles of beaches, roads, and trails today. If I had spent the whole day on Highway 101, I would have gotten to this same point by walking 18 miles. The Oregon Coast Trail isn't efficient, but it is interesting.

Day 23
Friday, August 10

Last night we drove back to Gold Beach to spend the night at the Sand and Sea Motel. This morning is another beautiful sunny day. Karen dropped Dionne and me off at Burnt Hill Road and we walked on Highway 101 for only a short distance to the beginning of numerous trails that start just north of and continue on through Samuel H. Boardman State Park. The park runs most of the distance between Pistol River Park and Brookings with trails a good portion of the way from one end of it to the other. But the trails are intermittent, so you're never on a section too long before it comes back out to the highway. You may have to walk on the road for a while or it may be just a matter of walking to the other end of a parking area to get back on the trail again. We were not able to get good trail maps of this area or good information on the condition of the trails.

What we found was that the trails at the north end of today's hike were in bad repair, overgrown with vegetation (blackberry bushes), poorly marked and nearly impassable. My recommendation for hiking this section is to carry a machete and wear leather pants. I was wearing shorts and my legs got pretty scratched up. From Arch Rock on, the trail improves significantly and the views are spectacular. In my opinion, the section of the Oregon Coast Trail between Pistol River Park and Bandon is the most scenic.

This beach goes nowhere but it's worth visiting.

The hike is fantastic, but we are having some logistical problems. The map we got at the information center shows a parking area that doesn't appear on a different map that we just got from a park ranger. Karen is supposed to be waiting for us at a wayside that may not exist, and we have no cell coverage to make contact and change plans. We aren't going to let that bother us too much. The scenery here is too spectacular to be bothered with logistics. What is there to see along here? Beautiful coves surrounded by cliffs with rock islands, natural arches, and secluded beaches. All this is framed with lots of green vegetation and conifer trees. You are unlikely to find yourself entirely alone in this area but it's anything but crowded. Most people are concentrated a short distance from parking areas so there is plenty of space to be alone.

Another spectacular view.

The trail brings us up near a wayside so we go up to see if it's the one where Karen is supposed to meet us. I don't see her car but Dionne finds a note from Karen left at 1:05 p.m., just 20 minutes ago.

> *"Ken and Dionne, I am returning every 30 minutes on the hour and half hour. I am trying to get cell phone service but I think my battery charger isn't working so if all else fails, I'll meet you at the Bon Motel in Brookings."*

It is 2:00 now and we've traveled 10 miles so far. Karen showed up on schedule and we ate lunch and switched hikers. Dionne is now in the car and Karen is on the hike. It isn't long until we are at the Thomas Creek Bridge. I believe it is the highest bridge in Oregon. Everything bad I said about the trails at the far north end of the park are more than balanced by the fantastic experience we are having along the mid-portion of the park.

Not long after I decided the trail was fantastic, it turned against us. We met a major obstacle at the south end of Whaleshead Beach. At this point we had traveled 15 miles and it was 4:15. The direct line distance to House Rock Viewpoint where we were to meet Dionne was just a little over a mile away. It would take us over an hour to get there. The north end of the trail has been wiped out by a slide. Apparently they didn't know about this at the information center and the ranger we talked to earlier today didn't tell us about it either. Maybe ignorance is bliss. If we had known, we would have had to walk on a section of road.

Karen at the base of the landslide.

I took the lead climbing up the slide area and worked my way up to a pretty bad spot which was quite steep and covered with loose rock, so there wasn't much to get a grip on. I used my trekking poles for stability and worked my way across it and then climbed about 20 feet farther up the trail to a more secure place to stand. I looked back to see how Karen was doing.

Karen is clawing her way up the slide zone.

She was coming up the slide on hands and knees, making good progress until she got to the steep spot with the loose rock. She started across but lost her grip, and inch by inch began to go down the chute. She was in danger of sliding all the way to the bottom. I told her to jam her hiking pole into the ground below her and put some of the load on it. That stopped her for the moment, but she was unable to move from that spot.

Karen is stuck. She can't go down or up without sliding down the hillside.

I faced a moral dilemma. Should I risk my life and go back over that same dangerous spot again to save her or, realizing that the worst case scenario wasn't that bad, stay up here and save myself? If I don't help, the worst that could happen is that she falls to her death and I become the sole recipient of our parent's estate and my revenge will be complete.

Against my better judgment, I did go back to help her get across. I hope I don't regret this in the future. It was so contrary to the goal of inviting her on the trip. On the other hand, she did look pretty scared and that was worth a lot.

We continued up the trail, which clearly hadn't been used for a while and was overgrown with vegetation. Eventually this trail intersected with another and we found that the trail we had just come up was closed at the south end. We continued south on the intersecting trail. It was about 5:15 when we arrived at the House Rock Viewpoint, where Dionne was waiting.

It was getting late in the day and we were still a little over five miles from Brookings by road. Who knows how far it would be if we continued on trails? It took an hour to complete the last mile and we don't know the condition of the trails south. So even though I have avoided being goal-oriented up to now, we decide that the best approach to the next leg of the journey is for Dionne and Karen to drive back to the motel and I will carry a light pack and run along Highway 101. It is 5:35 now and it shouldn't take me much more than an hour to cover the distance.

Running to Brookings on Highway 101.

The run to Brookings was a little hilly but not bad and I enjoyed jogging along, covering ground at what felt like breakneck speed compared to hiking on the trails. As I entered Brookings I passed by South Coast Lumber Company, which I toured just a few months ago in my previous life as a sawmill engineer. I'm enjoying this trip much more than that one. At 6:30, 55 minutes from when I started running, I arrived at the Bon Motel. I hiked, crawled, and ran 22 miles today.

The journey is nearly complete. It is just 7 miles from here to the California border. We're all hungry and a victory dinner is in order. We find a restaurant that has steak and potatoes. After dinner we return to the motel and go to bed early so we can get an early start in the morning. We intend to complete the walk and then drive back along Samuel H. Boardman Park and stop at a few places so we can hike in and see the views that Dionne missed when Karen was with me and that Karen missed when Dionne was with me.

Day 24
Saturday, August 11

The battle between being goal-oriented and experience-oriented is over. Today it is all about the goal. No attempt to find a trail or walk the beach, we will walk the seven miles through Brookings to the California border on the shoulder of Highway 101. We wake up early and are ready to go at 5:40 a.m. It's cool and dark when we start. Dionne and I are walking and Karen will meet us there with the car.

After two hours of walking we can see the California border. Karen is waiting for us at the green highway sign that says "Welcome to California." Balloons are attached to the sign and a finish line ribbon is stretched across the two posts. About fifty yards from the border I start running for the final sprint to the finish. Wait . . . . that ribbon looks like it might be wrapped around a steel cable and it's about neck high and Karen is encouraging me to run faster. I throw caution to the wind, throw my arms up and break through the ribbon. There is no steel cable. Apparently she has no hard feelings about the suffering I've put her through on this hike. She has champagne and treats set out for us. Where are the helicopters and the news media? We celebrate for a bit and I add my signature to many others on the signpost.

Finish line!

Adding my signature, champagne in hand.

EPILOGUE

I WALKED THE ENTIRE length of the Oregon Coast. It won't go down in the history books but I feel that it is a significant accomplishment and it was a great experience. I not only spent some good quality time with nature, but I also got to have the company of my youngest son Chris, my running partners Michael and Charlie, my wife Dionne, and my sister Karen.

As to the original plan of inviting my sister, I think it was a complete success. The numerous face-plants, the bruised leg, the twisted ankle, the fear of death at the landslide, and the ordinary aches and pains (of a woman of her age) tackling a journey of this magnitude was revenge enough. I feel that I have completed my mission and the bitterness of my youth is gone. There will be no need to invite her on another adventure. On the other hand, maybe I will. It was a lot of fun.

Thanks to:

Many anonymous local folks who gave me directions and advice on accommodations.

The family from Wyoming for providing a boat ride across Nehalem Bay.

Andrea and Larry for providing food, housing, good company, and a ride to the north end of the Bayocean Peninsula.

Chris, my youngest son, for spending some good quality time with his old man and for helping me cross Cascade Head, the most challenging section of trail.

Chris's friend, Trenton, who picked Chris and me up in Waldport and drove us to Corvallis.

The family at Lincoln Beach who invited us for dinner at their family reunion.

My running partners, Michael and Charlie, who gave me a ride from Portland back to Waldport and provided me with good company for a couple of days.

Jeff, the harbor master at Winchester Bay, who made arrangements to get Dionne and me across the Umpqua River.

Jeff and his wife, the campers at the mouth of the Umpqua River, who offered Dionne and me a little rest, refreshment and a ride across the Umpqua in their boat.

The helpful man at the Charleston Visitor Center.

A taxi driver who drove out to the middle of nowhere and took us back to our car when we had a family emergency.

The camper at Floras Lake who gave us a bag of fresh strawberries. They were soooo good.

Sue at the Gold Beach Visitor Center who made a trail map for us.

My sister Karen, who put up with her irritating little brother for a week and provided logistical support, entertainment, inspiration, and a great celebration party at the California border.

Dionne, my wife. Where do I start? She was the original inspiration for this trip. I have lived in Oregon for 35 years and I had never heard of the Oregon Coast Trail. Dionne found a pamphlet describing the trail and said, "This looks like it would be fun." I looked at the information and was hooked on the idea. Unfortunately, her schedule only allowed her to walk some portions of the trip but she had a huge part in making the trip happen. She drove me to the mouth of the Columbia River where I started this hike and she drove the car to southern Oregon for the ride home and made a number of support trips in between. She came to the coast to visit me on rest days and she walked with me for eight of the 23 hiking days. She was always supportive and really made the hike fun.

Total miles hiked: 466
Total number of hiking days: 23
Average miles per day: 20

Disclaimer: This journal is a record of what life was like for my companions and me on the Oregon Coast Trail. If you want to use this journal as a hiking guide, forget it. All turns, locations, distances, names and descriptions of places, and other "facts" found in this journal are probably wrong.

—Ken Patton

Epilogue to the epilogue:

Sadly, my husband Ken died suddenly and unexpectedly in December 2011. He had compiled his journal entries and photographs into a narrative, making it possible to publish this account of one of his many adventures. The inconsistencies between present and past tense reflect the nature of journal writing and were not edited out in order to preserve his voice. My good and generous friend Ginny Jensen helped me prepare Ken's story for publication.

—Dionne Bradley

ABOUT THE AUTHOR

Ken earned a Bachelor of Science degree in mechanical engineering from Portland State University and raised his three children in Portland, Oregon. As a professional engineer, he designed sawmill equipment for Crow Engineering and later Weyerhaeuser. He achieved his long-term goal to retire at age 55 and directed his artistic and mechanical talents to creating kinetic metal sculpture. Within a few years his work was recognized and exhibited locally and internationally. His *Mesmerometer* is on display at Oregon Museum of Science and Industry in Portland and his triple pendulum sculpture *Tourbillon* is installed at Boonshoft Museum of Science and Discovery in Dayton, Ohio. He loved planning ambitious adventures including hiking and cycling the length of the Oregon coast, cycling across Oregon, and kayaking from Portland to Astoria. Ken planned to create art, hike, kayak, and ride his bike forever.

kenkinetic.com
YouTube channel - kenkineticart